AF441965

MULTIMEDIA INTERACTION WITH COMPUTERS
Human Factors Issues

MULTIMEDIA INTERACTION WITH COMPUTERS
Human Factors Issues

JOHN A. WATERWORTH, B.A., Ph.D.
Institute of Systems Science
National University of Singapore

ELLIS HORWOOD
NEW YORK   LONDON   TORONTO   SYDNEY   TOKYO   SINGAPORE

First published in 1992 by
ELLIS HORWOOD LIMITED
Market Cross House, Cooper Street,
Chichester, West Sussex, PO19 1EB, England

A division of
Simon & Schuster International Group
A Paramount Communications Company

Printed and bound in Great Britain
by Bookcraft, Midsomer Norton

British Library Cataloguing in Publication Data

A catalogue record for this book is available from the British Library

ISBN 0–13–605429–3

Library of Congress Cataloging-in-Publication Data

Available from the Publishers

Contents

Preface 11

Acknowledgements... 15

Chapter 1 - Introduction... 19

Chapter 2 - The Process of Design 31

Chapter 3 - The Content of Design 49

Chapter 4 - Hypermedia: Current Concerns, Future Directions......................... 71

Chapter 5 - Analogy and Dynamism in Multimedia Design............................. 88

Chapter 6 - Exploring Multimedia Information.................................113

Chapter 7 - Usability Assessment: Two Case Studies.................................140

Chapter 8 - Desirable Futures?...174

Bibliography...188

Index 207

Detailed Table of Contents

Preface 11

Acknowledgements 15

Chapter 1 - Introduction 19
1.1 BACKGROUND 19
    1.1.1 A Shift of Focus 19
    1.1.2 Multimedia Interaction with Computers 20
1.2 A HUMAN FACTORS APPROACH 21
    1.2.1 Designing for Usability 21
1.3 HYPERMEDIA, PROBLEMS AND PROSPECTS 23
    1.3.1 Modes, Models, Metaphors and Magic 23
    1.3.2 Visualizing the Future 24
1.4 MULTIMEDIA APPLICATIONS AND USABILITY 25
    1.4.1 Hypermedia and Other Applications 26
    1.4.2 Usability Assessment 26
1.5 TOWARDS THE FUTURE 27
    1.5.1 Where are we going? 27
    1.5.2 A New Religion 29

Chapter 2 - The Process of Design 31
2.1 EXPERIMENTAL PSYCHOLOGY AND HCI 32
    2.1.1 Introduction 32
    2.1.2 What is a User Interface ? 33
    2.1.3 Human Information Processing 34
2.2 THE ROLE OF INTERFACE DESIGN 37
    2.2.1 Usability 37
    2.2.2 What is HCI Design? 39
2.3 EVALUATION 41
    2.3.1 Aims and Metrics 41
    2.3.2 Behavioural Evaluation and Experimental Psychology 42
        2.3.2.1 Variables and Control 44
    2.3.3 Locus of Evaluation 46
    2.3.4 Conclusions 47

Chapter 3 - The Content of Design...**4 9**
3.1 TASK ANALYSIS FOR DESIGN...49
    3.1.1 Introduction...49
    3.1.2 Talking to Potential Users...51
        A. On the representation of history...52
        B. On interpreting city planning...52
        C. On lecturing...53
        D. On writing/research...54
        E. Archive staff...55
    3.1.3 An Example of the Design Process...55
    3.1.4 Concluding Comments...57
3.2 DESIGN GUIDELINES...57
3.3 PROTOTYPING...61
    3.3.1 Alternative Approaches to Prototyping...61
    3.3.2 Rapid Prototyping Tools...62
    3.3.3 New Developments and Trends...65
        3.3.3.1 Interface Specification...65
        3.3.3.2 Construction Kits...66
        3.3.3.3 Incorporating Knowledge...67
3.4 SOME DESIGN OPTIONS...68

Chapter 4 - Hypermedia: Current Concerns, Future Directions...**7 1**
4.1 INTRODUCTION: INTERFACE DESIGN FOR HYPERMEDIA...72
    4.1.1 Issues from Conventional Interface Design...72
    4.1.2 Empirical Studies of Hypermedia Usability...74
    4.1.3 Summary of Design Issues Specific to Hypermedia Systems...76
4.2 DIRECTIONS FOR FUTURE RESEARCH...78
    4.2.1 Approaches to Usability...78
    4.2.2 The Empirical Approach...79
    4.2.3 The Anthropomorphic Approach...81
        4.2.3.1 Conversational Interaction...81
    4.2.4 Visualizing Hypermedia...83
    4.2.5 Using Hypermedia in the Future: key issues...84
        4.2.5.1 Relevance...85
        4.2.5.2 Importance...85
        4.2.5.3 Selective Views...86

Chapter 5 - Analogy and Dynamism in Multimedia Design...**8 8**
5.1 INTRODUCTION...88
5.2 METAPHORS IN INTERFACE DESIGN...89
    5.2.1 Levels of Metaphor Mapping...92
    5.2.2 Problems with Metaphors...93
    5.2.3 The Use of Metaphor in Hypermedia...94
5.3 DYNAMISM IN HYPERMEDIA...97
    5.3.1 An Example Application...98
5.4 DESIGNING INTERFACES: PROBLEMS AND EXAMPLES...100
    5.4.1 Why is Design Difficult?...100
    5.4.2 Example Interfaces...102
5.5 CONCLUSIONS...110

Chapter 6 - Exploring Multimedia Information **113**
6.1 INTRODUCTION...113
6.2 A THREE-DIMENSIONAL MODEL OF INFORMATION EXPLORATION 115
   6.2.1 Structural Responsibility 115
   6.2.2 Target Orientation...115
   6.2.3 Interaction Method..117
6.3 PARADIGMATIC EXAMPLES OF INFORMATION EXPLORATION 118
   6.3.1 Navigational Browsing 119
   6.3.2 Navigational Querying..120
   6.3.3 Mediated Browsing 121
   6.3.4 Mediated Querying...122
6.4 EXPERIMENTAL COMPARISON OF FOUR EXPLORATION STYLES 123
   6.4.1 Materials 123
   6.4.2 Subjects and Method 124
   6.4.3 Results 125
   6.4.4 Discussion..126
6.5 DEVELOPING INFORMATION EXPLORATION SYSTEMS 127
   6.5.1 Hypermedia and Information Retrieval..127
   6.5.2 Index Linking...131
   6.5.3 Patterns of Exploration Behaviour...133
      6.5.3.1 Starting...134
      6.5.3.2 Chaining...134
      6.5.3.3 Differentiation...134
      6.5.3.4 Monitoring 135
      6.5.3.5 Extracting and Evaluating...135
      6.5.3.6 Target Specificity...136
6.6 CONCLUSIONS 137

Chapter 7 - Usability Assessment: Two Case Studies...**140**
7.1 INTRODUCTION...140
7.2 ASSESSMENT OF A COMPLETE CAI PACKAGE...141
   7.2.1 Description of the Software...141
   7.2.2 Aims of the Evaluation 142
   7.2.3 Practical Constraints on Timing and Approach...142
   7.2.4 Evaluation Method 143
      7.2.4.1 Introduction..143
      7.2.4.2 Assessment of Students' Performance..144
      7.2.4.3 Assessment of Students' and Instructors' Attitudes 144
      7.2.4.4 Expert Assessment of Software...144
      7.2.4.5 Quality of Instruction Methods and Guidance..................................145
      7.2.4.6 Quality of Design..145
      7.2.4.7 Quality of Program..145
      7.2.4.8 Quality of Training Content 146
   7.2.5 Summary Evaluation and Design Recommendations 146

7.3 RESULTS OF CAI PACKAGE EVALUATION..147
   7.3.1 Introduction: two trials...147
   7.3.2 Assessment of Performance with Scenario Questions...148
      7.3.2.1 First Trial...148
      7.3.2.2 Second Trial...148
   7.3.3 Results from Student Attitude Questionnaire...149
      7.3.3.1 First Trial...149
      7.3.3.2 Second Trial...151
   7.3.4 Expert Assessment of Program...152
      7.3.4.1 Observations on Software...155
      7.3.4.2 Expert Evaluation Summary...155
   7.3.5 Summary of Findings and Design Recommendations...156
   7.3.6 Summary Recommendations..158
7.4 COMPARISON OF MANUAL AND AUTOMATIC HYPERMEDIA LINKING 159
   7.4.1 Introduction..159
   7.4.2 Experiment One: Assessing Evaluated Relevance of Links 161
      7.4.2.1 Method..161
      7.4.2.2 Results..162
   7.4.3 Experiment Two: Assessing Predicted Relevance of Links 163
      7.4.3.1 Method..163
      7.4.3.2 Results..164
   7.4.4 Discussion..165
APPENDIX 1..166

Chapter 8 - Desirable Futures?...174
8.1 THE IT REVOLUTION: HERESIES AND DOGMAS...175
   8.1.1 Introduction..175
   8.1.2 Heresies and Dogmas of the Information Age...176
      8.1.2.1 Heresies...176
      8.1.2.2 Dogmas..177
8.2 VISIONS OF A VIRTUAL FUTURE..178
   8.2.1 Information City...178
   8.2.2 An Institutional Example 181
   8.2.3 Comments...182
8.3 VIRTUAL WORLDS: THE BEST AND THE WORST OF EVERYTHING 182
   8.3.1 The Redundancy of Literacy 183
   8.3.2 Everything is Possible, Virtually...184
   8.3.3 More for Everyone (who can afford it)...186

Bibliography...188

Index 207

Preface

The focus in this volume is on multimedia interaction, with particular reference to hypermedia. Despite promising a book on the discourse level of linguistic interaction (see preface to Waterworth and Talbot, 1987), a purely language-based approach now seems rather narrow and I believe that the richer conception of multimedia interaction is needed to contribute to the mainstream of work in information technology (IT) in the future. I also increasingly feel that what is possible by the application of artificial intelligence and computational linguistics to human-computer interaction is much more limited than has been claimed by many, and that this undercuts any general attempt to move beyond the surface level of interaction to the discourse level. I now believe that greater progress will arise from increasing the points of contact at the interactional surface, by which I mean enriching the flow of information across the interface between computers and their users. Multimedia is, more than anything else, the embodiment of this process of enrichment.

My intention in creating this book is both to give an introduction to and to cover the leading edge of research on multimedia human-computer interaction (HCI), from a human factors perspective. The content falls squarely in the category of HCI, not AI, Computational Linguistics, Cognitive Science nor its poor relation 'Cognitive Engineering'. Multimedia systems are a major research focus here at the Institute of Systems Science (ISS), where I have been based since leaving British Telecom in 1988. This has put me in a good position to track technical developments while working on the human use of such systems. However, the perspective on multimedia interaction presented here is my own; it is deliberately idiosyncratic and is not that of ISS. I do not attempt to provide comprehensive coverage nor to reflect any general consensus of opinion in the field.

Technical aspects of multimedia, and the way such technology is being applied, are covered in a set of two edited companion volumes. The first of these has already appeared (Waterworth, 1991), and looks in detail at the underlying technological requirements for multimedia applications to be developed. This provides explanation and expansion on the technological issues mentioned, but not discussed, in the present book. The second volume will focus on current and future applications of the technology, merging the purely technological aspects with those relating to human use, from a practical perspective.

Multimedia will be central to developments in IT over the next few years. Hypermedia systems are being extended to include not only text and images, but graphics, video, animation, and sound recordings. Such systems will be applied to a broad range of applications from education to entertainment, and including specialized systems for military, archiving, research, and other purposes.

This boom comes about from the development of optical disk technology for high volume storage, and the availability of high quality graphics and imaging at reasonable costs and fast processing speeds.

The other push is from the integration of several media into telecommunications systems, which will (fairly) shortly carry live video images alongside fax, data and speech transmission, with the widespread adoption of ISDN (Integrated Services Digital Network). In the longer term, telecommunications, computing, and information systems will merge. Questions of how different workers can cooperate and collaborate to do shared work via such systems then become vitally important.

Interest in multimedia from industry is broadly based; publishing, education, military, on-line information suppliers, telecommunications, entertainments concerns are all possible users of the technology. All of these developments raise numerous usability issues, centring around how the various media can be accessed by the user in an optimal way to carry out real tasks. This is the main subject matter of the text. There is also fairly detailed coverage of the methods used to bring about usable multimedia systems. This will be of interest to those with little or no background in the design and evaluation of human-computer interfaces.

Conversation is a good candidate as a model of HCI. Addressing this goal of 'natural dialogue', we observe that conversations are characterized by built-in robustness, rapid response times, and flexibility. And they are also, less obviously, multimedia in nature; speech, grunts, sighs, nods, eye contact, facial expression, pointing, showing, drawing, proximity, etc., may all play a part. With the availability of 3-D modelling, display, and manipulation devices, together with the capacity for rapid interactive access to multimedia databases, we are witnessing the emergence of the necessary technology for multimedia conversation between people, and between people and systems.

Most of the multimedia work in this book has been carried out in the context of so-called hypermedia systems. Hypertext has generated a lot of excitement, and a good deal of hype, as a new way of structuring knowledge (i.e. text) non-sequentially. Actually, there is nothing new about non-sequential access to information. But burgeoning hypertext excitement has resulted in a more flexible way of thinking about user access to information. And while the term hypermedia implies some degree of non-sequentiality, it increasingly includes almost any technique that allows flexible access to information. Hypermedia is simply multimedia hypertext. Given the loose definition of what hypertext is, almost any multimedia system can be viewed as hypermedia. For the purposes of this book I use the terms more or less interchangeably unless I am making a specific point about the distinction. Hypermedia should then be regarded as a sub-set of multimedia, with some degree of non-linearity in the way that information can be accessed and explored.

For readers interested in access to hypermedia materials, and particularly for those who would like to compare traditional text with hypermedia, an interactive version of this book has been prepared. Readers interested in gaining access to this hypermedia version of the text should contact me at the address given below.

John A. Waterworth
Singapore, March 1992.

Institute of Systems Science
National University of Singapore
Heng Mui Keng Terrace, Kent Ridge
Republic of Singapore 0511.
(john@iss.nus.sg)

Acknowledgements

First and foremost, I thank Mark Chignell of the University of Toronto, for supplying large quantities of "boilerplate" used to construct the fabric of several chapters, and contributing many of the ideas behind the experimental studies and the conceptual analyses. Without his major contributions, this would have been a very different, poorer and much thinner book.

I am also very grateful to the following people for their help:

Past and present members of my (variously named) research group at the Institute of Systems Science, National University of Singapore (ISS) most of whom have now moved on: Gurminder Singh, Chung Tze Min, Tng Tai Hou, Law Chee Keong, Sue Bowles, Geoff Nicholas and Raymund Chan, for their numerous contributions to the work that underlies this book. Similarly to past and present members of what was once the Hypermedia research group at ISS, especially Chua Tat Seng, Luis Serra, Koh Toh Tzu, Elaine Lai and Joel Loo.

Bernd Nordhausen of ISS for his work on the HEFTI project (Hypertext Extraction From Text Incrementally) and the link usability experiments carried out as part of that project. J Felix Valdez, currently a graduate student at the University of Southern California, for his contribution to the HEFTI model and to the usability experiments. Professor Dan Patterson and Peter Kellock, both of ISS Education Division, were very helpful in creating manually authored hypertext for comparison purposes.

Malcolm Murphet, Professor Peter Dennis, Professor Scott Dupree, and other interviewees, for the insights gained of the methods of information gathering and organization for scholarly research and of the rhetoric of teaching.

Staff of the National Archives and Oral History Department, National Museum of Singapore, who provided information on the organization and display of archival materials as well as access to those materials.

All the good people who "volunteered" to be subjects in the experiments described here.

The in-house editors at Ellis Horwood who corrected the manuscript with great thoroughness. Any remaining errors are my responsibility.

I thank the following for permission to use previously published material, including the reproduction of figures:

Chapters 4 and 5 incorporate material that was first published by Taylor Graham in *Hypermedia 1(3)*, 1989. Chapter 6 uses material published by Taylor Graham in *Hypermedia 3(1)*, 1991. Chapter 7 includes material published by the Human Factors Society in the Proceedings of their 35th Annual Meeting, August 1991.

to my parents

Chapter 1

Introduction

"All we have is words."

Samuel Beckett.

In this chapter I discuss the importance of our main topic, multimedia interaction, the scope of the book, and preview some of the topics to be explored. As described in the preface, the book in some ways follows on from a previous volume in the same series (Waterworth and Talbot, 1987). Certainly, the focus on the user's perspective and a firm belief in the value of the empirical testing of ideas have been retained. There is, however, rather less emphasis on technological concerns in the present case, and a more exclusive concentration on issues of HCI and usability.

1.1 BACKGROUND

1.1.1 A Shift of Focus

There is no doubt that the current high level of interest in multimedia interaction stems from recent technological developments. These developments are treated in depth in an edited companion volume (Waterworth, 1991). Here our interest lies in catering for users' task needs and preferences, in the design of interaction structures and strategies for multimedia applications. We develop this theme by drawing on the current literature in the field, much of which comprises practical appraisals of user needs, though some is somewhat theoretical and may not have been applied to quite these areas of interest before. There is a general lack of rigorous empirical work in relation to multimedia interaction. I report our own work in this area where it adds to the development of my theme.

This book represents a shift in focus away from interaction based purely on speech and other natural language, which reflects my current interests and work as well as a trend in research and development as a whole. A major change is taking place in the way computers are used and in their capabilities, a change that may be summed up in one suitably synthetic phrase: multimedia interaction. This development frees the computer user from his traditional diet of text, simple graphics, and more text. Multimedia interaction is incredibly exciting. Luckily for people like me it is also fraught with problems in the way in which it is implemented in relation to users' aims, tasks and preferences. It may also have serious social and cultural consequences.

1.1.2 Multimedia Interaction with Computers

The future of IT lies in multimedia systems. Owing to a variety of factors, such as falling costs of computing machinery, advances in digital techniques, development of optical disks, high resolution displays and other technological devices, the integration of several media in future information systems has become inevitable. This integration of sound, music, animation, text, narrative, video, images, and graphics is attractive in itself. But what gives the new computer-based technology enormously enhanced appeal compared to, say, television or video cassettes is the added dimension of interactivity.

Multimedia systems will proliferate in many applications, including communications, education, publishing, entertainment, and reference systems of a wide variety of kinds. Authoring, teaching, collaborating, and guidance software, amongst others, will play a key role in supporting activities in these areas. A critical factor in determining the user acceptance of this technology will be its usability in realistic settings. In a sense, more media means more problems. In this book I focus on issues of multimedia interaction with computer systems. That is, on the many problems and prospects for human use of the emerging multimedia technologies, not on the technologies themselves.

Recent experience has shown that IT must be easily usable to be successful; adequate functionality is necessary but no longer sufficient to guarantee success. The most obvious interaction issues relate to the way information is displayed to the user, whether this be as text, photographic images, animation, graphics, speech, video, or a combination of these. Many researchers have laid down guidelines for presenting information to users of systems, especially in the visual modality. But interaction concerns cover not only presentation but the whole gamut of exchanges that comprise human-computer dialogues. This includes not only what users see and when, but also how they convey their choices, selections, queries, commands and requirements; in fact the complete pattern of transactions they enter into, as a function of their needs, abilities, preferences, and experience.

1.2   A HUMAN FACTORS APPROACH

Chapter 2 introduces the approach being taken by human factors specialists (and others who would not describe themselves as such) to try to maximize the match between system designs and the needs of users and the tasks or activities they may wish to carry out.

While guidelines and research findings exist, so do large and significant gaps in knowledge. This is partly due to the inherent problem of predicting how system features will succeed or fail in realistic task settings, but also because the advent of multimedia interaction is raising truly new issues and problems. More than ever, iterative design and testing methods are necessary. No guidelines exist for the use of mixed media forms under multimodal control, and an empirical approach is the only solution. This method of developing successful designs is the main focus of Chapter 2 - The Process of Design.

1.2.1   Designing for Usability

Put as simply as possible, the aim of human factors work is to increase the usability of interactive systems. Usability can be measured in terms of the time to complete useful work. Overall time for a significant interaction is often referred to as transaction time, composed of finer-grain durations to complete component operations. Transaction time has proved to be one of the most dependable and meaningful measures for speech recognition systems, for example (Peckham, 1984). Other measures include the accuracy with which operations can be performed, user satisfaction in working with the system, and time to learn and retention of knowledge over time (Shneiderman, 1987a).

System usability is a function of several factors. An efficient system is one where tasks can be completed quickly, with minimum effort. There is now general agreement that consistency enhances usability, though it can conflict with other desirable characteristics, such as flexibility. A consistent interface will always use the same conventions for displaying information and for interacting with the system, across a range of similar situations. Recently, the value of systems that maintain consistency across applications has been recognized. But flexibility, allowing alternative ways of interacting to achieve the same effect, can also be desirable, by allowing expert users to take short-cuts, for example.

Although there has been a rather short-lived vogue for mixed-initiative systems in some circles (e.g. Bobrow *et al.*, 1977), the importance of allowing the user to be the 'boss' in the interaction should be recognized. Negotiation to clarify possibilities can be valuable, but a decisive user should be able to take the initiative with short, simple actions that achieve his purposes (see also Winograd and Flores, 1986). Users should immediately be aware of what they have done and its consequences, i.e. immediate feedback is necessary. The system should also be forgiving, allowing mistakes to be undone as far as is feasible, and not hiding effects, or trapping users in dead ends or infinite loops.

If the techniques of display and interaction seem natural to users, the system will obviously be more readily understandable. Another consequence will be increased ease of learning, including speed, transferability to the rest of the system, and retention of acquired skills over time.

Usability problems reduce user productivity and hence business efficiency, customer satisfaction and staff morale, profits and, in some applications, safety. Systems with low usability have an inhibitory effect on the market, and so reduce the potential for technological development. Yet vendors have only recently started to take usability seriously, and many users find their computers hard to use. Fortunately, designing for usability is now taken very seriously indeed, as witnessed by IBM's recent moves to share in Steve Jobs' NeXT ideas.

In Chapter 3 - The Content of Design - I focus on ways of deciding what to include in a particular multimedia application. These techniques include task analysis, incorporating ideas from published guidelines, and various approaches to prototyping design ideas.

As the interactive component of systems becomes ever more sophisticated, through the incorporation of more media and modes of control and feedback, the programming effort involved in specifying this component grows accordingly. User interface management systems (UIMSs) and other specification tools provide a variety of techniques for automating parts of this large task, and so make the design-test-redesign philosophy more practical.

1.3 HYPERMEDIA, PROBLEMS AND PROSPECTS

Chapters 4 and 5 focus on, amongst other topics, the problem of combining a range of input and output possibilities in an integrated, comprehensible way. Issues here include not only the media used, but the modes of interaction embodied using those media. The context is the development of hypermedia systems, a subset of multimedia typified by non-linear linking of nodes of information. Hypermedia is currently being applied widely, in education, entertainment, and information systems. Chapter 4 deals with current usability concerns arising from the adoption of hypermedia, and describes the ways in which future developments are likely to improve the situation. We discuss exactly what hypermedia is or is not, examining some of the overblown and dismissive claims and counter-claims that have been made. The problems of navigating complex information spaces and of information retrieval from multimedia systems generally are a major topic of discussion.

A key aspect of developing usable multimedia is the notion of conceptual models designed into interfaces by their creators, and the actual mental models that develop in users' minds as they interact with the systems. One way of breaching the gulf that tends to form between the two is through the use of analogy. Interface metaphors are one way of providing consistent models for both designers and users (though not necessarily the same one), by tapping real-world knowledge. But how close should the analogy be? Is it sensible to throw away computer power to conform to real-world limitations? And how should these 'as if' worlds be represented ?

1.3.1 Modes, Models, Metaphors and Magic

We can view interaction as a game, rather like chess, with rules and an agreed goal (not a good analogy, though, since achieving the goal in chess is hardly a cooperative aim). Alternatively, a joint expedition, under user leadership, to reach a desirable, but not necessarily agreed, destination might provide a better outlook on the issues. In this activity the system and the user each have different skills and moves that they are able to make, both within and across different media.

It is always important to remind ourselves that the way users think about a system is not the same as the way a designer will think about the same system. To the user, the interface *is* the system, and he has a view of the structure and functionality of the system that depends on his encounters with the interface, and past experience with other systems and the world in general. The consequences of a mismatch between these views is one major reason for early and repeated interface evaluation.

A recent trend to improve the adaptiveness of users' models of systems, and to increase compatibility with the designer's intended model, is that of incorporating so-called metaphors within interface designs. The most common example is the 'desktop' direct manipulation display. A more recent development in this direction, aimed at avoiding the problems of switching between different activities on the same workstation (while avoiding a cluttered desktop), is that of Rooms (Card and Henderson, 1987). The basic idea is to use different 'rooms' for different tasks (mail, control office, debate, etc.) enhanced with metaphor-consistent features such as Room redecoration, Doors and Back Doors, suites of Rooms, and pockets for carrying items from Room to Room.

The rationale of designing a computer system in terms of one or more metaphors is that this capitalizes on the user's world knowledge to help him understand the way in which the system works. If an interface display looks and, to some degree, works like a filing cabinet, for example, the user will not need to learn much to know how to file and retrieve documents. So need for learning is minimized through predictability in terms of how real world objects behave. Also, imposing the same metaphor across operations creates consistency of operation, thus increasing transfer of learning, and fewer errors will be made with this kind of intuitive behaviour. There is evidence that providing users with a metaphorical model, versus giving procedural instructions, to carry out a task leads to improved efficiency and memorability (e.g. Payne, 1987). But a metaphor will not match the operation of a system in all respects; adopting an inappropriate one is potentially very counter-productive (Halasz and Moran, 1982). Chapter 5 deals with the use of analogy and dynamism in multimedia design.

1.3.2 Visualizing the Future

Inherent in the use of metaphors is the portrayal or representation of the seemingly real. For example, one way to enhance the ease with which a complex knowledge base can be explored is by representing it as a 3-D structure through which the user could navigate. The characteristics of the structure would be designed to enhance memorability and appropriateness to information content. One experimental project,

SemNet (Fairchild *et al.*, 1988) uses techniques from flight simulation to create an artificial reality comprised of abstract graphical objects corresponding to a hypertext knowledge base. Users can explore this 3-D space as if it were reality, bringing the benefits of prior knowledge of navigating new environments (such as identifying landmarks, and travelling at varying altitudes to obtain views with different levels of detail). Added to this are additional powerful features (the 'magic' aspect of the new reality), such as instant travel to a selected part of the network.

A good deal of work is now being done on the use of artificial realities, often called 'virtual worlds' in this context, for visualizing and experimenting with scientific phenomena (see Brooks, 1988). The power inherent in the capability to produce interactive, sophisticated models of complex natural phenomena should not be underestimated, and this is a vitally important area for multimedia interaction research. Here the intimate relationship between display and input devices on the one hand, and choice of interface metaphor on the other, has already become clear. Rather obviously, 3-D presentation only works if the tools exist for adequately displaying and manipulating that representation.

Another example of similar recent developments in multimedia interfaces is the Alternative Reality Kit (Smith, 1987). ARK is a visual programming environment to create interactive animated simulations. The simulations provide alternative, artificial realities where the laws of nature can be explicitly manipulated. The interface is strongly metaphorical, with the laws of nature taking the form of visual objects. Smith discusses the trade-off between features that correspond to the metaphorical model the interface is built around, and 'magic' features that deviate from that model and so reduce learnability, but provide extra, sometimes vital, power. He also points to the importance of 'external' factors, unavoidable features which are neither magical nor metaphorical, as the most difficult for users to cope with.

The issues of visualization and the use of analogy are obviously intimated related and not without problems, to say the least, for the interaction designer.

1.4 MULTIMEDIA APPLICATIONS AND USABILITY

Multimedia work is gradually attracting the attention of more and more researchers, educators, and systems people as time goes on. The emerging technologies that are making multimedia interaction a feasible approach to an expanding range of applications are becoming ever more accessible.

1.4.1 Hypermedia and Other Applications

The problems of hypermedia are fairly well known (see, for example, Halasz, 1988), but the solutions to those problems are less clear-cut. The key issue is that of finding relevant information: not missing important items, not duplicating existing ones or entering details in inappropriate places, returning to interesting items at will, and so on. Allied to this is the need for structure in the information base, and for different views to be available depending on the type of user, his task or interests at a particular time. There is also a need for navigation of the available information by the user, which is a defining feature of hypermedia systems, to be augmented with techniques for system-mediated searches.

Chapter 6 - Exploring Multimedia Information - addresses this issue of how to design multimedia systems, rich in information and flexibly structured, in such a way that users can actually make use of that information. The chapter describes a model of the various ways in which users may attempt to extract information from a multimedia system, as well as an experiment comparing users' success with different styles of information exploration with different kinds of task.

1.4.2 Usability Assessment

I have already made the point that usability of systems is central to the success of the IT revolution. Interaction design for multimedia systems is likely to be driven by the need for 'naturalness', implying efficiency and ease of learning, and suitability for users' task-related needs and preferences.

An empirical approach is vital to successful dialogue design. Earlier chapters describe how this approach can be facilitated by subsystems for interface specification and prototyping, both general purpose user interface management systems and more specialized construction kits and design environments. New techniques for dialogue specification are already emerging. Fine-grain analysis of the best way to use several media, alone and in combination, is now needed.

While interaction design has been, and always will be, something of a black art, incorporating testing as part of the design cycle returns a healthy empiricism to usability work. In Chapter 7, I describe two evaluation exercises in detail. The first is an overall evaluation of a multimedia computer-aided learning (CAI) program developed for a military training application. I provide a specimen report on the evaluation of the system, to give the reader a practical insight into the techniques and materials used. The second case study is of a finer-grained analysis of detailed aspects of a system; specifically, a comparison of different linking strategies from hypermedia creation. Both types of evaluation, global and local assessment of features, will be needed to successfully develop future multimedia applications.

1.5 TOWARDS THE FUTURE

1.5.1 Where are we going?

Despite the recent explosion of interest in multi-window systems, icons, and other graphics-related issues, interaction design is not yet being tackled from a viewpoint that allows the increasing array of interaction devices to be integrated with users' tasks and purposes. The interactions are, literally, two-dimensional. User and system view each other through a window against which the user's nose gets flattened.

The aim is to open the window to a wider world of interactivity made possible, and probably essential, by the added dimension of multiple media. Only a very few attempts have been made to enter the user's world through multi-dimensional interactions (which would take account of work aims and structures, sequences of actions, meaning and effects in context). Multimedia is important, not only because of the new possibilities it opens up for presenting information, but because it is multi-channel. Multi-channel input from the user is just as vital as multimedia output.

Conversation naturally includes speech, grunts, nods, eye-contact, eyebrow movement, smiles, touches, showing things, pointing, even bodily posture. Far too little has been done to allow people make use of their inherent capacity to communicate and act in a multi-modal fashion, although new interaction devices are beginning to open up these possibilities.

For optimal interaction it is not so much a case of needing lots of built-in intelligence, as a need for *embeddedness* in the current situation, and the means to respond to cues, to be flexible, configurable, and responsive. Only users have purposes, and our claim is that the focus of systems design work should be on helping people fulfill their purposes, in the ways they want to, flexibly, as the situation unfolds, in an engaged way. This is what we all do, naturally, in conversation. Ultimately, we are still moving towards the idea of the conversational computer, but it is a richer form of interaction than one based on only the written or spoken word.

It is currently unclear, however, exactly which media should be used, for what, in what combination, and when. As Alty (1991) points out, we know a few things about the advantages and problems of using particular media for different types of task, but our knowledge is far from complete. Alty suggests that purely auditory presentation can be better for recall of dialogue than if the visual modality is also utilized, whereas action is better recalled from a presentation which includes visual material. Diagrams seem to be better for conveying ideas, but text may be better for detail. Alty presents Marmollin's characterization of when to use concrete or text-based representations of information (see Figure 1.1)

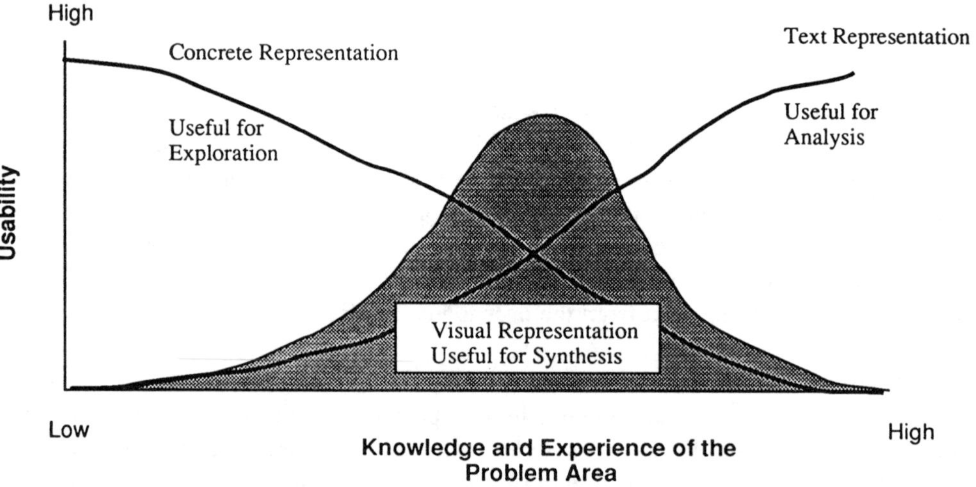

Figure 1.1 - Possible uses of different media (after Marmollin; in Alty, 1991).

Another issue is the method of interaction employed by the user. Requesting information from a system, perhaps by means of a textual query in standard information retrieval style, is very different from exploring a visually presented 3-D scene. Generally, the medium in which a user interacts with the system is known as the modality - speech, vision, touch, etc. - whereas media refers to the media of presentation to the user. Rather confusingly, the term multimedia may imply more than one medium of presentation, utilization of multiple sensory modalities of users, or both.

1.5.2 A New Religion

Multimedia systems are at the crossroads of three major technological trends: computing, informations systems, and telecommunications. Systems that integrate these three powerful elements will have an impact on daily life more than equivalent to that of the introduction of telephones, television, and computer games combined into one. Application areas such as education, cooperative work, authoring, entertainment, military command and control, information access, and ideas generation will all benefit from these developments.

Treating system entities and procedures as if they were objects in the world, while including necessary and additional features to provide functionality and extra power in use, amounts to creating new realities in which users carry out tasks, express themselves, learn by discovery, and are entertained. The emerging technology of hypermedia, where a large, multiply-linked web of multimedia information can be explored in a great variety of ways, is one major area where artificial realities are likely to become commonplace.

The way in which people use systems is changing, through the development of new, integrated styles of interaction, incorporating both conversational and direct-manipulation aspects. This is particularly important for the successful use of multimedia systems. Artificial realities, metaphors and new interaction devices will extend the usability, scope and excitement of emerging multimedia systems.

Metaphor at the interface is here to stay, but the real world will clearly not limit the scope of artificially created worlds. We are no longer slaves to a system-dominated world of technical languages and arcane procedures; we are on the brink of becoming masters of our own magical reality. In Chapter 8 I present one vision of what the coming artificial realities might look like, where metaphor and magic combine with new interaction devices and navigational styles.

There is great promise, but also some danger here. A vast virtual reality which is consistent, in its own terms, and like the real world in lots of ways is also a place where the impossible becomes possible. Instant visits to interactive video 'places', discussions with (the semblances of) historical figures, communications with any and everyone on a world-wide broadband network, creation of works of great beauty, and of monsters, battles with other people, spells and potions, alliances and treachery, death and re-birth, discussion, argument, wizardry, and all deeds undo-able.

This is 'value-added' reality. It will be unimaginably engaging: art and science merged in a compelling evolving environment in which we all work and play and express ourselves. The dangers lie in the effects this has on the real world around us, on the physical and human world in which we live. What if the metaphor mapping process reverses and we come to think (sometimes unconsciously) of the real world working as if it is the virtual one, and the virtual world becomes real? I conclude with a speculative discussion about the impact of this 'new religion' on society at large.

Chapter 2

The Process of Design

"Think of the design process as involving first the generation of alternatives then the testing of these alternatives against a whole array of requirements and constraints."

Simon (1981)

In this chapter I open our discussion of the issues involved in designing efficiently usable multimedia applications. I start with what I consider to be the originating discipline for the scientific approach to interactive design: experimental psychology. This is followed by a consideration of the process aspects of interaction, and of interactive design. Task analysis is outlined as a key element of this latter process; guidelines form another important component. Designs must be tested and it is often advantageous to use rapidly produced prototypes or simulations to speed an iterative cycle of design, test, and redesign. After discussing techniques and tools for prototyping and evaluating interface designs, I lead into the larger topic of the options open to the designer of multimedia applications.

2.1 EXPERIMENTAL PSYCHOLOGY AND HCI

2.1.1 Introduction

The empirical study of HCI is rooted in experimental cognitive psychology, which has been well defined as follows:

"Cognitive psychology is the scientific analysis of human mental processes and structures with the aim of understanding human behaviour" (Mayer, 1981).

The important point about this definition is that it stresses the need for scientific analysis and includes both processes and structures.

What then has cognitive psychology to do with HCI design and evaluation? There are three main points of contact. Firstly, information about human characteristics is needed to guide design towards features that are compatible with: memory capabilities, attentional limits, perceptual characteristics, the nature of human learning of facts and skills, and physiology. Secondly, the methods of cognitive psychology can be used to evaluate designs and user interface (UI) features. Such areas as experimental design, statistical testing of hypotheses, interview and survey methods can be applied to the comparison of alternative designs and to examine the effects of manipulations or time. Thirdly, there is an intrinsic similarity between the design of experiments and the design of UIs. Both are iterative, and at various stages, neither is ever perfect, and both involve trade-offs such as applying cost constraints versus a more nearly ideal solution, or in the application of conflicting principles and guidelines.

I can go a stage further and briefly discuss the notion of isomorphism between the system with which a person is interacting and the psychology of that person. Both multimedia systems and, as we have seen from the definition of psychology cited above, human users can be studied in terms of information structures and processes. It is possible to view the quest for usability as the search for ways of matching two information processing systems: the multimedia application and the human user. It is sometimes claimed that since, as far as we know, human knowledge is organized as some kind of loosely structured network of associations, similar non-linear arrangements of multimedia information, through which authors and readers can travel at will according to their interests at any particular time, will have advantages over more traditional forms of information organization. This is, in essence, the claimed advantage of hypermedia over linearly organized material.

The problem with this claim is twofold. Firstly, we do not know much about how information is organized in the human mind. Secondly, what we do know we cannot use introspectively; human information access from storage is by and large an automatic and unconscious process. There is no self-evident reason that information organized in a similar structure would be of benefit to people in accessing information. There is no direct channel or means of communication that could effect a mapping between the two information systems, human and machine. We rely on standard human capabilities for interacting with the environment in all HCI. The channel is narrow and the mechanisms are general purpose. Information documents and tools of various kinds ('document' here includes poems, plays, films, catalogues, etc.; 'tools' includes indexes, bookmarks, photocopiers, fast forward buttons, etc.) have been developed to capitalize on human capabilities. It could be argued that we should look to traditional forms in our attempt to develop appropriate multimedia documents and information tools, rather than engage in the quest for some mythical direct mapping of information between systems and their users.

Let us move on to consider, firstly, what is meant by a UI and, secondly, the nature of human information processing and how that impacts on what goes on at the user interface,

2.1.2   What is a User Interface ?

We can characterize an interface as a communication channel between two agents that are cooperatively performing a task. One, the actor, carries out actions as a result of behaviours selected by the other, the behaver. If the initiative is shared between system and user, these roles will alternate, but my preference is to regard the user as most likely to be the behaver, and the computer system as the actor that responds to those behaviours. The components of an interface can be described with the following mnemonic (ABCDEFG):

- Actions
- Behaviours
- Contexts
- Displays
- Effects
- Forms
- Goals

The *behaviours* selected by the behaving agent lead to *actions* performed by the acting agent. The behaviours and actions that can occur are defined by *contexts*. One of the central tasks of interface design is to enforce appropriate contexts and to provide appropriate cues to the behaving agent as to which contexts are available at each point in time.

Displays are outputs of the interface that are designed to be read or viewed for their own sake. Text fragments, charts, and pictures are all examples of displays.

Effects are feedback provided to the behaving agent that indicate the consequences of behaviours within the form of the interface.

The *form* is the representation of task activity that is conveyed by the interface. For instance, the Macintosh Finder Desktop is a form. Dragging a file into the trashcan is a behaviour, modifying the shape of the trashcan is the effect, and tagging the file for deletion is the action.

Finally, it is the *goals* that motivate the behaviours that have to be handled by the interface. Any interface design that does not include a thorough analysis of the task goals is bound to fail.

2.1.3 Human Information Processing

Underlying user interface design and cognitive psychology is the view that people are purposive processors of information. Usability issues revolve around active information processing and capacity limitations that are axiomatic to cognitive psychology. These characteristics of the human system supply some of the basic parameters for UI design. Figure 2.1 illustrates a simplified view of the human information processing system.

The model suggests that the human processing system acts both as a filter and as a buffer of information. Items identified (unconsciously) from the information registered by the senses are stored very temporarily in immediate store (IS). IS has the curious property that more can be stored there than can be reported. Ingenious experiments by Sperling (e.g. 1960) showed that around 16 visual items could be stored in IS for about 0.5 s, although only about 4 of these 16 items could be reported at any one time. For sound stimuli, the retention period is a little longer, at up to about 4 s. This limit on what can be reported is due to the fact that, to be reported, the items must be transferred to the seat of consciousness, short-term store (STS). STS (also referred to as working memory) is the limiting factor in the whole system.

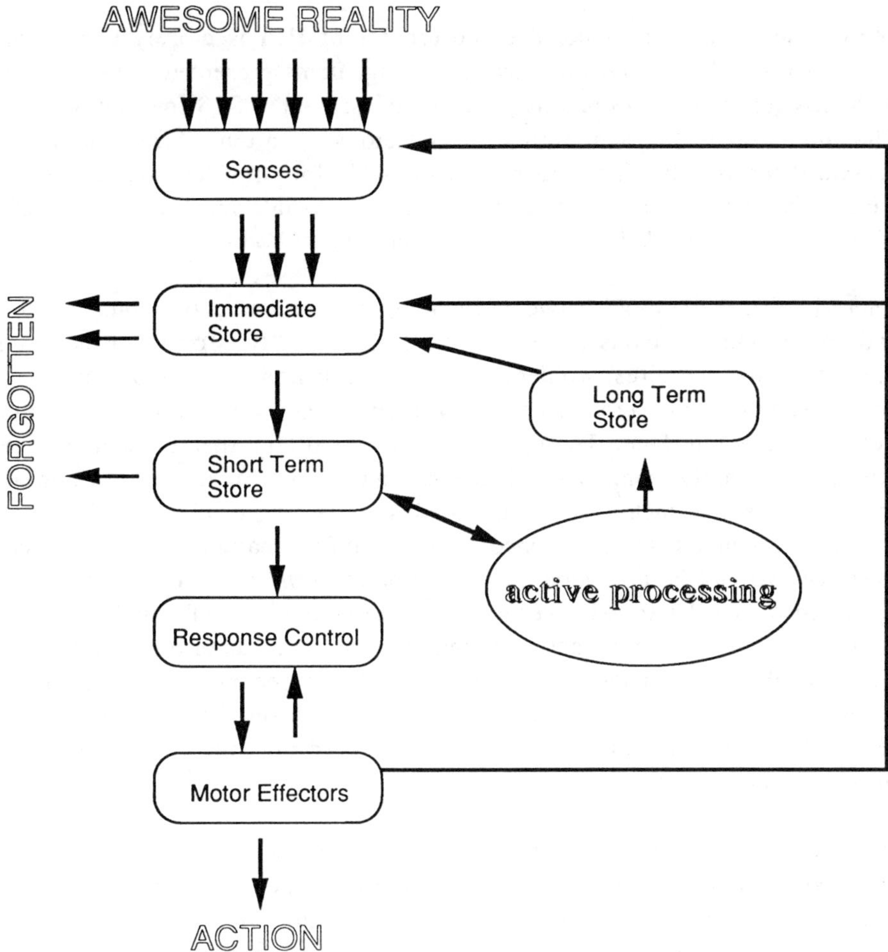

Figure 2.1 - Human information processing model

STS can be equated with those aspects of information processing of which the individual is normally conscious, and this constitutes the bottleneck in human information processing. The number of items that an individual can attend to, or actively retain for conscious processing, is limited to around seven (Miller, 1956). Such attention or retention is an active process, it takes conscious effort. Long term store (LTS) is of virtually unlimited capacity, though recall is not always successful. Items stored here represent well learned skills, information, or experiences: the great bulk of human memory. Recalling items from LTS involves locating and transferring them to STS so that they are accessible to consciousness and can then be acted upon.

We can see from this model that the process of HCI is closely connected to the mechanisms of human information processing. Items presented at the interface will be briefly registered in IS and may then be transferred to STS for conscious attention. The limitation is the availability of conscious attention. If too many items are presented too briefly, they will not be available for consideration. Decisions taken while information is held in STS will result in new information being transferred to LTS or to behaviours being carried out by the user, or both.

There is also a trade-off between attending to new items presented to the senses and performing conscious processing on those items. If information is presented to the user which requires problem solving or decision making of some kind, this comprises information processing that will reduce the extent to which he notices new events at the interface. Therefore, if it is important that those new events be attended to rapidly, some way of interrupting his information processing activities may be necessary, such as a sound stimulus or flashing display. By the same token, a user who is in a state of vigilance, looking out for a particular event to occur at the interface, will not be in a good position to perform information processing activities. Evidence for the balance between stimulus sampling and information processing in the distribution of attention can be found in estimates made of the time spent carrying out particular types of task (Waterworth, 1984). In general, time spent on a task is judged to be relatively long when the emphasis is on detecting new events, and relatively short when the emphasis is on carrying out mental processing on previously detected events.

Procedures which the user has to follow should be easy to learn (easily transferrable to LTS), should make use of the user's existing and easily recallable knowledge (easily accessible from LTS), or the information needed to carry them out successfully should be presented or obtainable in such a way that it is readily available to conscious attention. Most of the issues of HCI design revolve around trying to make things easily usable, capitalizing on existing knowledge, or providing easily accessible information in an assimilable form when it is needed.

2.2 THE ROLE OF INTERFACE DESIGN

2.2.1 Usability

Usability is a necessity in any interface design; adequate functionality is not sufficient. The most obvious area for the application of usability criteria to multimedia interaction is in the presentation of information. Equally important are the processes by which the user exercises control over the systems: the choices, selections, commands, and queries that comprise his dialogue with any application software. Although there has been a trend to attempt to embed increasing amounts of intelligence within the interface, to cater automatically for specific users and their needs, automation is not the complete answer by any means. Indeed, the quest for increased automation can lead away from our goal.

Our goal in developing interactive systems is not to make computers more powerful but to make people more productive. This becomes increasingly clear as we move from text-based systems with a narrow band of interactive possibilities, to multimedia systems with much broader potentials for interaction. In terms of machine intelligence, multimedia technology is no different from earlier text-based systems. But in terms of human use the change is revolutionary and demands corresponding changes in interaction styles.

We can assume that computer power, in terms of the ability to store data and perform computation, will be adequate to our needs in the future. The question is, how much of this power can be utilized by people ? At its simplest, utility can be seen as the ratio of value over effort; our aim then is simply to increase the value of our users' behaviours, while decreasing the effort needed for them to achieve their purposes.

HCI design is in many ways the subject of paradoxical considerations. The more complex and sophisticated we make technology, and the more it simplifies nature, the more complicated it will be to learn and to use. Although many users are enthusiastic about new technology, they do not want to have to learn new ways of working; they simply want to get their work done. Users will happily use suboptimal strategies if they achieve their aim and are easy to learn. It is difficult, if not impossible, to change the way someone uses a system once he has become familiar with a way of interacting that meets his needs. The scarce resource in interface design is human attention, not computer power. Additionally, we have the fundamental problem that neither users nor designers know what they need, at least in the early stages of a new design. We must ask them, nevertheless.

High usability has often been regarded as a function of the following eight factors: efficiency, consistency, flexibility, feedback, user initiative, openness and forgivingness, understandability, and learnability. Efficiency means simply that users can complete their tasks quickly, with minimum effort. Most people agree that consistency in the way information is displayed and of interaction methods is a good thing, both between and within applications. However, consistency may conflict with other desirable features such as flexibility, and should not be followed slavishly. If it can be achieved without compromizing the needs of a particular application, it should be aimed for. Flexibility can be contrasted with consistency to some extent, since it involves providing alternative ways of interacting, for example, for experts and novices. This need not always compromise consistency but is quite likely to do so, particularly if the needs of particular users or a very specific application are being addressed.

The provision of feedback is a key element of a successful interface. Quite simply, users need to know what the consequences of their behaviours are as soon as possible. It is also important, as far as possible, to give the user the initiative in the interactive process; this is closely related to the issue of feedback, since retaining initiative depends on tracking moment by moment activities at the interface. Another 'user-behaviour-centred' aspect of usability is the design of open and forgiving interfaces. A user cannot make sensible decisions, cannot hold the initiative in a meaningful way, if the consequences of behaviours are hidden. Nor should the user be able to arrive at interactive situations from which there is no escape, i.e. there should be no dead ends and no infinite loops. If the techniques of display and interaction seem natural to the user, then the design will be much more understandable and successful. An important consequence of this is learnability. As far as possible, the skills and knowledge needed to interact with a system should be quick and easy to learn; and preferably such knowledge will be transferrable between applications.

We can see that usability of interactive systems boils down to two related considerations: maximizing the effectiveness of users' behaviours, and, maximizing the users' importance in the interaction. Despite the notion of user-system isomorphism alluded to earlier, the concept of usability implies an inherently unequal relationship between the participants at the interface. We should not forget that we are serving the needs of the user, not developing interesting machines for the sake of it.

Multimedia interfaces present several interesting problems for the designer whose aim is high usability. Multimedia systems may contain a very large amount of information in, by definition, several different media such as text, 2-D and 3-D graphics, animation, images, video, sound (including narrative, music, and effects). Issues arise from both the volume of material, and its diversity in terms of media and informational content. Because the material in a multimedia application may be heterogenous and therefore linked in a complex way, both authors and readers are required to take on an active role in navigating the resultant structures, hence the need for sophisticated information tools. In a sense, such interfaces place users directly within the informational structure they are creating or exploring. The need for this intimate involvement with structure partly determines the way in which interfaces are realized. Tools are also needed to allow users to access and control material in different media. A particular difficulty is how to deal well with dynamic media such as video and audio. Can and should the tools for these media be very compatible with those for the more traditional static media such as text and images? More detailed aspects of the usability of multimedia systems such as this are covered in Chapter 6.

2.2.2   What is HCI Design?

HCI design is actually the beginning rather than the end of the software design process, and interface design should continue throughout software development and testing. The requirements for the software should be driven by the needs of the interface rather than vice versa, that is, the software should be pulled from the user's needs rather than pushed from the technological capability. This is often not the case.

As we saw with our opening quote from Simon (1981) HCI design is, above all, an empirical process. In essence, this is also the philosophy behind the experimental approach of cognitive psychology, the alternatives being hypotheses about human mental functioning, yielding predictions that can be tested experimentally.

The idea of an iterative design-test-modify interface development cycle is almost universally recognized as the only reliable route to successful user interface design, though it is not broadly applied because of practical constraints such as limited budgets or limited time before a project must be completed. There is also considerable scope for variation in the way in which it may be approached.

Figure 2.2 shows three main aspects of the UI design cycle. Firstly, user/task analysis and modelling; secondly, prototyping of various kinds, both rapid and full scale; and finally, evaluation, at various stages and using a range of techniques. I discuss these three aspects of design in the following sections.

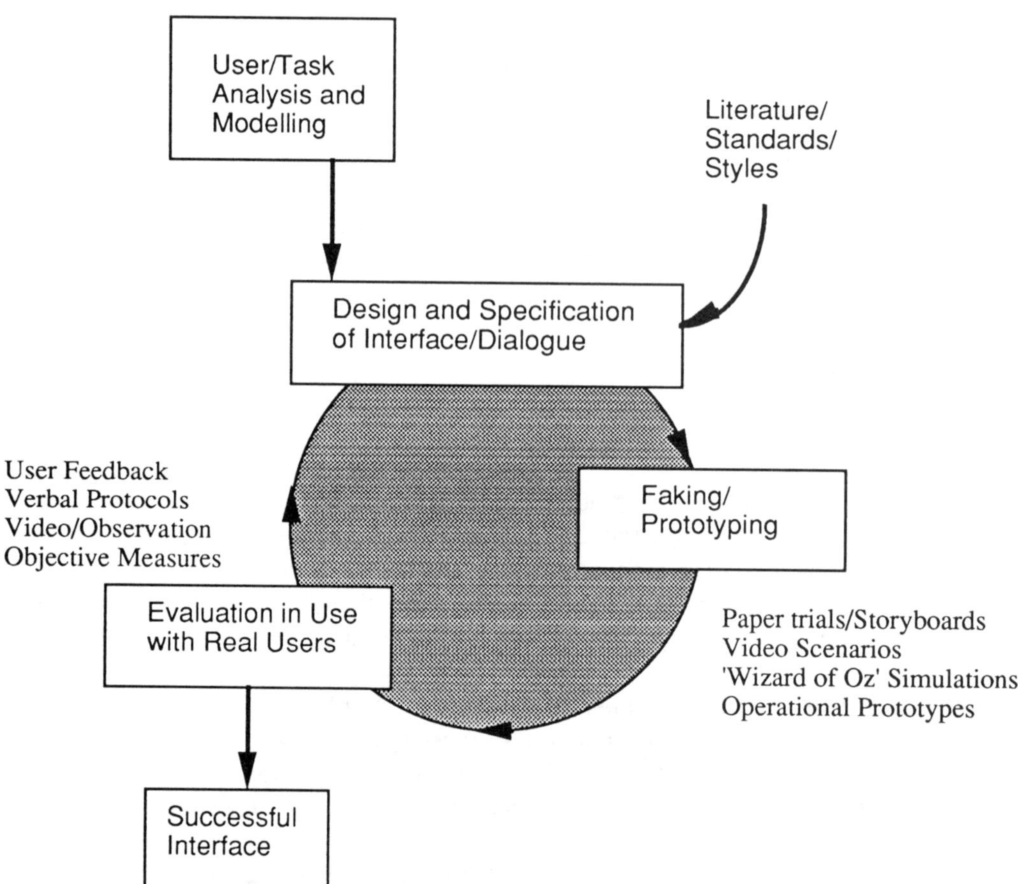

Figure 2.2 - UI design cycle

Identification of user characteristics answers the basic question "Who are the users?". We need to know whether we have an homogenous group of users, or different identifiable skills and roles to meet. What are the skills, ages, and pattern of use? Is there a hierarchy that will determine access and other privileges? Other important factors are the level of motivation of users and the extent they will be willing to cooperate with the design process. Most important of all is the question of what task or tasks users will wish to achieve with the system being developed, hence the need for a task analysis perspective on design.

2.3 EVALUATION

2.3.1 Aims and Metrics

Evaluation is concerned with the measurement of usability, either globally in terms of task performance, or at a more fine-grain level to assess individual features of a design. Usability can be equated with utility for a given task which, as I mentioned earlier, is proportional to value, where value is the amount of productive work carried out; and is inversely proportional to the effort users put in to carrying out a particular piece of work. Usability has also been described as a function of efficiency, low error rate, and user satisfaction (Shneiderman, 1987a).

There are a great many metrics that can be applied to the assessment of usability. A popular and seemingly valid measure is that of transaction time; that is, the time to complete a particular task (e.g. Peckham, 1984). The similar work speed metric is based on the measurement of percentage of task completed per unit time. Other frequently used metrics include the ratio of successes to failures, time spent on errors, percentage and number of errors, number of commands used, frequency of access to help and documentation, percentage of favourable versus unfavourable user comments, number of times users need to work around a problem, number of times users lose control of the system, and number of times the users express frustration with the system.

Detailed behavioural trials, using real users performing realistic tasks, are needed to thoroughly assess the performance characteristics of prototype systems. Rigorous testing is also needed to test more specific hypotheses about detailed aspects of the interface. Videotaping and automatic logging of users' interactions are useful for identifying problem areas. Different design solutions are compared on the basis of measures such as transaction time and error rates. These types of measure have the major advantage that all user behaviour is recorded and data is accurately timed. Additionally, they interfere with neither the user nor the behaviour of the system, although care must be taken over the way video recording is used. Automatic logs can record data in a form that permits easy statistical analysis. These methods are often used in combination with other measures.

Post-encounter questionnaires are routinely used to gain an insight into users' subjective impressions of system performance, along with informal interviews. Objective results are usually analysed in detail and tested for statistical significance. Evaluation will often be carried out over a period of repeated encounters with the system, to assess ease of learning and any effects of fatigue. Recently, sophisticated metrics of usability have been developed to describe the complexity of different dialogues and to account for, or predict, the difficulty users will have with new interface designs (see Sharratt, 1987, for a brief review). Details of evaluation materials and methodology for a multimedia computer-aided learning program are given in Chapter 7.

An increasingly popular technique for early evaluation of candidate designs is protocol analysis. Here, test users provide a verbal protocol of their experiences with the system, by 'thinking aloud' about what they trying to do as they interact with the simulation (Lewis, 1982). Structured diaries, which trial users fill out after each encounter with a new system, are another way of assessing overall effectiveness of design (see Norman and Draper, 1986).

A recent paper by Cuomo and Sharit (1989) assessed a battery of different assessment techniques for users carrying out computer-aided architectural design tasks. Their discussion includes the conclusion that total task time can serve as an indicator of task complexity. They suggest that errors are primarily a function of the individual as reflected by his or her mental model of the system, the UI design, and the mental workload the user is experiencing. They also make the important observation that protocol analysis is the only reliable way to discover the cognitive strategies underlying users' behaviour. They suggest that the problem with objective measures alone is that different types of behaviour can produce the same effects; for example, backtracking to try something additional versus backtracking because of making an error.

2.3.2   Behavioural Evaluation and Experimental Psychology

The importance and relevance of this topic lies in the underlying idea of experimental test. To design a system that will work well in a particular task situation, it is necessary to try out possible features in practice - guidelines and recommendations are only one starting point, as I said earlier. To know which of two or more alternative designs works best in a particular situation with particular users it is necessary to compare them empirically - expert opinion is not sufficient. To find out what the strengths and limits of human skills and capacities are, we need to test people on appropriate tasks. And to develop models of human cognitive functioning we need to generate and test predictions about how people will behave in a variety of task settings.

In short, the experimental method is the cornerstone of cognitive psychology, and also of UI design. In cognitive psychology there is a solid body of findings that can lead to further refinement. In UI design very little is known that can be generalized - empirical testing is the key to success.

The experimental approach has several important components such as:

(i) identifying the questions to be asked, in the light of what is already known,

(ii) formulating hypotheses,

(iii) designing an experiment, considering factors such as variables, control, balancing, and subjects,

(iv) collecting data and the statistical treatment of results,

(v) drawing conclusions and reporting findings.

Cognitive psychology uses scientific methods to draw conclusions based on careful observation of human behaviour. A basic assumption is that any explanation of behaviour must be testable. In other words, it must generate predictions of what will happen in particular circumstances that can be observed. A basic tenet is that we can never know for sure that an explanation is true, we can only show that it is false. Following Popper, we assume that all scientific explanations must be falsifiable. Theories are hypotheses, not facts. They are only kept as long as they explain a wider range of behaviour than competing theories, or they are simpler than competing theories that explain the same phenomena, and they can generate testable predictions (that could, in principle, prove that the theory is false), and they have not been shown to be false so far. For *theories* we can substitute *designs*.

To qualify as an experiment, an evaluation would need to exhibit four essential features. Firstly, the experimenter must *manipulate* some feature of the situation. Secondly, this manipulation must be made under *controlled conditions*. Thirdly, the experimenter must *observe* the effects of the manipulation, i.e collect data. Finally, the effects, taken in the light of the manipulations, must have some *implications* for the issue in question, that is, they permit hypothesis testing. The factors present in an experiment are of two types, independent and dependent variables.

2.3.2.1 Variables and Control

The independent variable in an experiment is the variable systematically varied by the experimenter. We might be interested in knowing whether a mouse, a lightpen, or a joystick is best for a particular task. If the researcher varies which of these input devices the subjects use, and then observes the effects, input device is the independent variable, and in this case has three levels.

A dependent variable is a particular variable on which the subject's performance is measured. We might want to know how the choice of input device affects the speed with which a user can carry out a task, and also the number of errors he produces. Speed and number of errors would be dependent variables in this case.

The concept of control is based on the idea that you can only evaluate a result if you have something to compare it with, and that to make meaningful comparisons you should compare conditions that only vary in relevant ways (as far as this is possible). So, if we want to know how well people perform with System B, we need some other system with which to compare it, say, System A. And, if we want to compare performance on System A with performance on System B, it is not a good idea to use a colour display for A and a black-and-white monitor for B - we will not be able to tell if the difference is due to the system or to the monitor used. We have confounded the variables. And if we use female subjects for A and male for B, and our females are all considerably younger than our males, we have confounded four variables: system, display, sex and age.

The simplest experiment is where we have a control condition and one experimental condition. If we want to look at the effects of colour display, for example, then our control condition would be System A with a black-and-white monitor, and our experimental condition would be System A with a colour monitor.

Subjects in experiments (users in evaluations) can be a problem and need to be controlled very carefully. One reason for this is that they are all different. Another reason is that they learn. We need to make sure that, in comparing two or more experimental conditions, the results we obtain reflect the effects of our experimental manipulations and not the fact that the subjects we use are causing the difference. There are four approaches to controlling subject factors: (i) using subject variables as independent variables, (ii) using each subject as his own control, (iii) matching subjects, and (iv) randomizing subjects.

When we treat subject variables as independent variables, we deliberately manipulate the subject variable we think might be relevant, and examine the effect on the dependent variable. So we might compare a group of males with a group of females for each of two experimental manipulations, making four conditions in all. We can then examine the effect of our manipulation and the effect of sex separately. One problem with this approach is that it increases the amount of variance in performance that is due to subject differences, since every condition has a different set of subjects. This makes differences between conditions harder to spot.

One very economical way of removing the problems of different subject groups is to use each subject as his own control. This means that every subject experiences each condition, so that the subject groups between conditions are identical. This is known as a within-subjects or repeated measures design, whereas all other designs are known as between-subjects, because comparisons between conditions are also comparisons between different subjects.

The problem with within-subject designs is that experiencing one condition might affect how a subject behaves in another. In comparing ease of use of different sets of instructions for a public viewdata system, for example, we would not want to try all sets of instructions on the same user, since after the first, he would already have a pretty good idea of how to use the system.

We can control some of the problems of prior experience by balancing the orders of presentation of conditions, e.g Group 1 experiences Condition A followed by Condition B, Group 2 experiences Condition B followed by Condition A. But sometimes no prior experience is essential.

We are always concerned with comparing like with like. If we cannot treat subject differences as an independent variable, we should aim to equalize their effect across conditions. One way is by matching. Suppose we know that level of anxiety is an important factor in determining how well people detect the presence of aircraft on a radar display, along with the display technology used. We also know that learning to use the displays takes several sessions so that it is impractical to use a subject for more than one condition. We can test subjects for their anxiety level, but we are not interested in the effects of anxiety as such, and we expect a broad range of scores that would be difficult to allocate to groups. Our main interest is in choosing a display.

To match our subjects we can adopt the following procedure:

  • measure each subject on the variable in question before the trials are conducted

  • pair two subjects who have similar scores

  • randomly assign one subject to one of the conditions and the other to the other conditions

  • repeat until all subjects have been assigned to the two conditions

Using subject variables as independent variables, or using a matching procedure will still not take into account all possible subject variation. Furthermore, many cannot be measured. Using a subject as his own control is one way around this. When this is inappropriate, randomization provides an alternative. This simply involves numbering subjects, then using some system such as a random number generator to assign the subjects to each condition. If we have large enough groups, any subject variables should be distributed between groups in a random fashion.

Even when we use other procedures, such as matching, we should use randomization whenever possible, to remove potential biases of which we may be quite unaware. An experimenter might unconsciously allocate more intelligent-looking subjects to a particular condition, for example. Or, the first ten subjects who turn up may be physically fitter than the rest; they should not all be allocated to the same group. In our matching procedure we might invite our matched pairs to turn up for the experiment during the same time slot. Before the first subject enters the lab we would flip a coin to decide which condition to assign him to. The second subject would be allocated to the other, and so on for every pair of subjects.

2.3.3 Locus of Evaluation

Multimedia systems are complex, and they often exhibit little formal structure. The informational content of a large hypermedia system, for example, is distributed amongst heterogenous links that are richly, and unpredictably, interconnected. The interface model used to try to convey this spaghetti-like structure to the user inevitably tends to be arbitrary in character. In dealing with the informational content both authors and end-users are required to take an active role in navigation. In this sense, many multimedia systems place their users directly within the informational structure they are creating or exploring. The interface is not only at the level of an overall model, it is also distributed amongst all the information points a user might reach within the system. Given this complexity of interaction, several loci of evaluation should be considered, so that we can distinguish local problems from more general design deficiencies.

One way of evaluating local aspects of multimedia system designs is to embed assessment devices throughout our system. Nielsen (1990b) suggests the use of a 'reject' button at each node, which the user clicks to indicate that a particular link he has followed is useless. Taken a stage further, we can persuade groups of users to make a rating of link quality, on a sliding scale from, say, 'Very relevant' to 'Totally irrelevant' every time they follow a link. If we wish to be less intrusive, we can offer users a variety of types of link, and record which types are followed most frequently. Such data can be used to compare linking strategies, or overall hypermedia structures (see Chapter 7). Since most multimedia systems are aimed at providing information access, comprehension of that information by users is often a good indicator of usability.

A traditional evaluation, such as Shneiderman (1989), looks at a system more as an external 'over the shoulder' monitor than as an internal interrogator. While such studies can track the history of users' interactions accurately and so identify the well-visited nodes and the well-used features of the interface, they rely quite heavily on experimenter interpretation and on the assumption that frequently used equals well-designed.

2.3.4   Conclusions

By the methods described above we hope to arrive at an informed choice, to identify interface designs that reach an acceptable level of usability. The link between interface design and experimental psychology reveals itself particularly clearly in behavioural evaluation. As far as possible, good experimental methodology should be adopted. Specific hypotheses about the appropriateness of different dialogue features, in relation to the performance of particular interactive tasks, may also be tested, thus advancing the state-of-the-art of knowledge about HCI.

We cannot afford always to be as completely rigorous as the experimental method demands, nor is this always meaningful, especially during the early stages of prototyping. When using a paper mockup, for example, we are interested in obtaining quite informal feedback, not in precise behavioural measures. Even when we have a fully fledged implementation with which users can interact fully, we may initially opt for rapid evaluation using some of the less formal usability metrics such as verbal protocols. And often, economical or other practical constraints will lead us to rapid evaluation (Nielsen, 1990c). In early stages of evaluation we are basically debugging, looking for obvious errors in the way the interface is implemented. Also, we need to realize that results or observations are always influenced by contextual factors that will change with users' experience with new technology (see, for example, Whiteside *et al.*, 1988). But this should be a consideration that guides our evaluation design.

The view that the methods of experimental psychology are the key to successful evaluation of interactive systems is rather old-fashioned, and I do not wish to suggest that they are always feasible, nor that they of themselves guarantee a valid result. The main point I want to convey in this chapter is that we should use necessary means to iterate around the design loop, and we should use appropriate means according to the questions we are asking and the claims we would wish to make. Considering the experimental method will help us to avoid contamination of our tests and spurious conclusions. It will also force us to be precise in formulating the questions we expect our study to address, which is often not the case in informal assessment. There is no reason at all why a rigorous approach cannot take account of the insights currently claimed for more casual techniques.

Chapters 6 includes a brief report of an experiment conducted in the tradition of cognitive psychology, as part of the process of deriving knowledge to feed into the process of designing multimedia interfaces. Chapter 7 presents two evaluation case histories; one illustrates an experimental method for fine-grain 'local' analysis of a hypermedia system by means of the user-rated goodness of links, while the other includes description of a set of evaluation techniques applied to the detailed, but more global, assessment of a multimedia computer-aided learning program.

Chapter 3

The Content of Design

"If you choose to believe me, good. Now I will tell how Octavia, the spiderweb city, is made. There is a precipice between two steep mountains: the city is over the void, bound to the two crests with ropes and chains and catwalks. You walk on the little wooden ties, careful not to set your foot in the open spaces, or you cling to the hempen strands. Below there is nothing for hundreds and hundreds of feet: a few clouds glide past; farther down you can glimpse the chasm's bed.

This is the foundation of the city: a net which serves as passage and as support. All the rest, instead of rising up, is hung below: rope ladders, hammocks, houses made like sacks, clothes-hangers, terraces like gondolas, skins of water, gas jets, spits, baskets on strings, dumb-waiters, showers, trapezes and rings for children's games, cable-cars, chandeliers, pots with trailing plants.

Suspended over the abyss, the life of Octavia's inhabitants is less uncertain than in other cities. They know the net will last only so long."

- from *Invisible Cities* by Italo Calvino, p 61, published by Pan Books, London, 1979.

3.1 TASK ANALYSIS FOR DESIGN

3.1.1 Introduction

Task analysis is, amongst other things, the logical analysis of a task into a hierarchy of goals and subgoals, often yielding a rule-based description of subgoals and the identification of resources required by different subgoals. We are interested in the underlying purpose of tasks, relative importance and frequency, the sequence of operations within tasks, time-frames and the degree of inherent discontinuity, where the critical points in operations lie, what the locations are and associated environmental conditions, how instruction or learning by other means occurs, and whether or not tasks are carried out under the supervision of others.

Methods of gathering information include surveys, structured and unstructured interviews, informal or formal observation, and video recording for later analysis. All of these methods are used to arrive at a task characterization that forms the basis for further discussion about the nature of the operations we are concerned with facilitating through the development of a new multimedia interface.

Task analysis, and the resulting task model, comprises seven discrete steps:

1. Gather information

2. Format, condense and prioritize information

3. Conceptual analysis/design (semantic)

4. Dialogue level analysis/design (syntactic)

5. Input/output analysis/design (lexical)

6. Creating an interaction model (---> UI design)

7. Simulating, prototyping, testing

An initial approach to constructing multimedia interface designs for broadly educational applications was to step back and take a very general look at the sort of tasks, and possible interactive styles, that might be involved. For example, one topic of interest in our design work was the development of interactive history systems for students at various levels. We gathered views from several sources, trying, as far as possible in these initial interviews, to participate in and encourage the generation of possibilities rather than to narrow down to a very tight prescription of task structure. Interviewees at this stage included a professor of English (with active interests in history, the creative use of new media and technology and, as it turned out, the relationship of all these to architecture), history lecturers, authors and researchers, school teachers, museum curators and archive staff, amongst others. This stage was useful in stimulating our ideas regarding possible models of searching for, organizing, and synthesizing information of different types for various purposes such as research, education, training.

3.1.2 Talking to Potential Users

The following are summarized transcripts of a few of the tape-recorded interviews we conducted.

A. On the representation of history:

City planning in/as poetry
>>as modelling in space
>>with perspectives of...
>>outside-in for city
>>inside-out for poems.

Egyptology - possible users
>>specialists
>>archaeologists, historians, theologians
>>planners
>>general interest coffee-table "book"

Pyramid model/book model
>>working from both ends
>>content/index
>>>(glossary as part of index)
>>summary/review
>>series of parts in between

"the less you know, the deeper you go"
>>because the expert has a picture in his mind

hierarchies
>>word
>>topic
>>argument
>>conclusions/summaries
>>>(acting as guide)
>>>(with notetaking support)

Desirable functionalities
        replicate archaeological dig
                (cf flight simulator)
        paraphrasing/translation
                (for history of religion)
        inventory of every object
        'extend': explain further,
        in other media, more words,
        'refer': through background,
        in terms of context,
                (like arising from or giving rise to)

Purpose of project
        test the model
                (too cumbersome? too much information?)
        explore possible modes of information organization
                (as video game, as quiz review)
        explore some psychological aspects of book
                ('don't want to see' phenomenon, playful intent)

B.   On interpreting city planning

the what-if approach
arguments opening up into surprizes
non-interpretive nature
non-linear, non-logical
applied to poetry
        as medium for experience -
        'set of pouches'
        'media strips'
 as source of potentials

possible trends
        less writing and argument
        rhetorical, e.g. advertizing

ideas
> highlighting as foreground/background interplay
> composition as opposed to organization
> explore scale of clutteredness
>> (medieval writing has no title page: significance?)
> city states
>> have what in common ?

role play - ruler etc.
> to explore what-if, how-can
> metaphor - lab
> interface rule as function of information
>> changing information about rule

planner may want to know -
> look, shadow, noise level
> moving about the building

C.　On lecturing

classroom setup, lecture material
> where through maps,
> what through pictures
> need local examples that students can relate to

preparation - for good teaching
> organization/reorganization
>> (European history domain - non-hierarchical)
> chronological
> geographical
> by theme e.g. cold war

good students have interest and imagination

study of history
> real people
> material for thoughts

goals of teaching
>   a real appreciation
>   stimulate personal hunger
>   mental set correction
>   go back in time

act of teaching
>   a performance/ego-booster
>   an exercise of reaching out

D.   On writing/research

a hunt among the archives
>   a personal sorting through

setting themes
>   start with ideas
>   ideas shaped by material

collect material from several libraries/museums
>   personal visits helpful
>   on-line search convenient, but frustrating when
>   database not updated or complete
>   multimedia (photographs) important but not central
>   archives not arranged according to historian's needs
>   sometimes things are in the wrong/strange place
>   sometimes complete volumes eaten by mice

organizing collected data
>   transfer to notecards
>   (very time-consuming)
>   old-fashioned, use shoeboxes
>   chronological order
>   simple colour scheme for cross-referencing
>   not efficient

E. Archive staff

In talking to archive staff, we focused on the selection of application topics, on what would comprise an application of feasible scope, on how to arrange access to multimedia information on the topic, as well as seeking advice on classification and organization of the information, and the needs of clients who might use such an application.

Aside from such application-specific questions, I was concerned to establish the organizational and departmental setup, the current range of projects and the way workload is organized. Another concern was to establish who their clients were, and the process of deciding and carrying out a particular piece of work, such as an exhibition for schools.

3.1.3 An Example of the Design Process

The following simplified example illustrates the seven steps of task analysis/modelling as applied to the development of a multimedia history system for use by school children. The scope of the knowledge base was intended to be the history of Singapore during the Second World War, and would comprise text, graphics, animations, photographic images, and narrative sound recordings from survivors of the events at that time.

---

1. Gather information

Make video recordings of many hours of real enquiries to archive services; interview researchers, students and teachers.

2. Format, condense and prioritize information

Decide on the types of enquiries to be analysed and prepare tapes for rapid analysis, including verbatim transcriptions and summaries.

3. Conceptual Analysis

Identify general pattern of transactions and significant activities. In other words, arrive at answers to the questions, "What comprises a task, from the enquirer's point of view ?" and "How is a task completed?".

4. Dialogue Level Analysis

Identify ways of accomplishing significant activities within the task (enquiries, responses to enquiries, completion of stages), and

identify rules describing patterns of interaction for significant behaviours (such as combinations of moves/items for requesting and supplying information, organizing material, storing sets of material, recalling and modifying those sets).

5. Lexical Analysis

Identify individual lexical items used (items/moves - for selecting, confirming, cancelling, storing, requesting, etc.).

6. Creating an interaction model

The creation of an interaction model is an instantiation of the results of the analyses carried out at earlier stages. An interaction model is a prototypical user interface design.

7. Simulating, prototyping, testing

This is not a linear process and, as I have said, it will be iterative, occurring at several stages in the development of an interface. Every new application results in a repeated cycle through the steps above. So the prototypical interaction model is like a skeleton that is fleshed out, through following essentially the same steps, to produce particular instantiations of the model in specific application programs. For example, instead of gathering information about the form of information transactions, at these later stages we gather information that comprises the content of such transactions. And our multi-level analyses similarly focus on content as opposed to interactive form. The result is an actual interactive application that can be evaluated in a realistic task situation.

3.1.4   Concluding Comments

Task analysis provides a wealth of information to feed into the design process. As we have seen, other techniques that will often also be used include interviews with potential users, detailed discussions with 'focus groups' on the jobs they carry out, and the administration of directed questionnaires. But beware! Users generally are not capable of articulating the full complexity of what it is that they do, so that naturalistic observation is a much safer approach. Users are equally, or even more, unlikely to come up with good designs for new systems, though they can point to bottlenecks or other problems with current procedures. They also tend not to be aware of the potentials for creative design afforded by emerging multimedia technology.

Several techniques exist for task analysis, drawing on a range of disciplines that focus on patterns of behaviour and transaction. These methods of content analysis include conversational and discourse analysis, popular in linguistics as techniques for characterizing language events and the way they are achieved by interacting people in various circumstances (see Levinson, 1983). This approach has been successfully applied, for example, to define the regularities of interaction in conversations between expert providers of information and information seekers (Waterworth, 1989). Once characterized, a model of the process of information exchange for a given task can readily form the basis of designing an appropriate dialogue for automating the transactions involved.

3.2   DESIGN GUIDELINES

As potential designs are arrived at, reference should be made to whatever information already exists about specific details, drawing on experimental work reported in the literature, and on established guidelines. Many researchers have tested fine grain aspects of HCI. Details about how to incorporate specific media may be important. For more details see Brown (1986) and Marcus (1983). Numerous guidelines have been published, from the most general to the more specific, and several major vendors now have their own set of interface standards. While this is a generally positive development, there is a danger of stultification of the design process if excessive reliance is placed on standardization. Table 3.1 presents 25 primary guidelines, from a set of 45 culled from the literature by the Scottish HCI Centre (Alty *et al.*, 1986). Although several years old now, these signal points have not been superseded.

Table 3.1 - Primary Dialogue Design Guidelines
(letters in parenthesis refer to the source key below the table)

1. Use the user's model (A,B,C,D,F,G,I,J,K,N)
2. Be uniform and consistent (A,B,C,D,E,G,H,J,L,O)
3. Allow query in depth (B,C,D,E,H,I,N)
4. Make the state of the dialogue observable (A,B,C,D,E,N)
5. User should control computer (A,B,D,E,H,O)
6. Avoid acausality (B,C,D,E,I,L)
7. Allow single or multiple entries (B,C,D,H,I,N)
8. Provide reset command (B,D,E,G,J,M)
9. Be clear (avoid ambiguity) (B,E,F,H,J,O)
10. Be brief (B,E,F,H,O)
11. Allow input flexibility (B,E,H,I,N)
12. Log activities (D,E,G,I,J)
13. Be protective of user (A,B,E,M)
14. Let user control dialogue exchange rate (A,H,L,O)
15. Adapt to different user levels and styles (E,H,I,M)
16. Provide flexible checking mechanism (A,B,I)
17. Be relevant (B,F,H)
18. Introduce through experience (C,D,I)
19. Accommodate every possible user input (A,N)
20. Respond promptly (B,C)
21. Do not insist on optimal strategies (B,L)
22. Allow for intromission (B,L)
23. Allow user personalization of environment (B,N)
24. Provide backtrack facility (D,E)
25. Be constructive and positive in responses (K,M)

A	Bailey (1982)
B	Cheriton (1976)
C	Gaines and Facey (1975)
D	Gaines and Shaw (1983)
E	Gebhardt and Stellmacher (1978)
F	Grice (1975)
G	Hansen (1971)
H	Kennedy (1974)
I	Maguire (1982)
J	Pew and Rollins (1975)
K	Shneiderman (1982)
L	Thimbleby (1980)
M	Turoff *et al.* (1978)
N	Wasserman (1973)
O	Zimmerman (1977)

While there is a good deal of agreement about certain aspects of what constitute desirable interactive features, these tend to be of a general nature. For example, commonly accepted screen layout rules include the following proscriptions:

1   Do not clutter the screen

2   Do not display non-meaningful information

3   Do not be inconsistent

4   Do not display irrelevant information

5   Do not dazzle the user with too many colours

There is broad agreement about general guidelines, but their wide-ranging, but vaguely-stated, goals may not be measurable. This has resulted in a trend away from general principles and towards detailed layout style guides. Increasingly, the various large computers companies are issuing their own sets of guidelines for graphical, direct manipulation (e.g. Apple, 1987). These will ensure consistency and a certain brand 'look and feel'. But in trying to apply guidelines it is important to remember that there is no universal set of design goals. Different systems have different aims, and this will affect what is appropriate at the user interface. Also, many sets of guidelines are available, and these are often inconsistent or conflicting. They are also very incomplete in terms of the facets of interaction that they address, but it may not be clear what has been omitted until we try to apply them in practical situations.

Empirical work is still needed to determine what works best for many aspects of a particular interactive situation. And there is still an element of 'black art' in interface design, even when as much information as possible has been gathered. There are usually many ways of achieving the same aims in a design. Therefore no one design is 'right', and all designs have pros and cons that must be traded off.

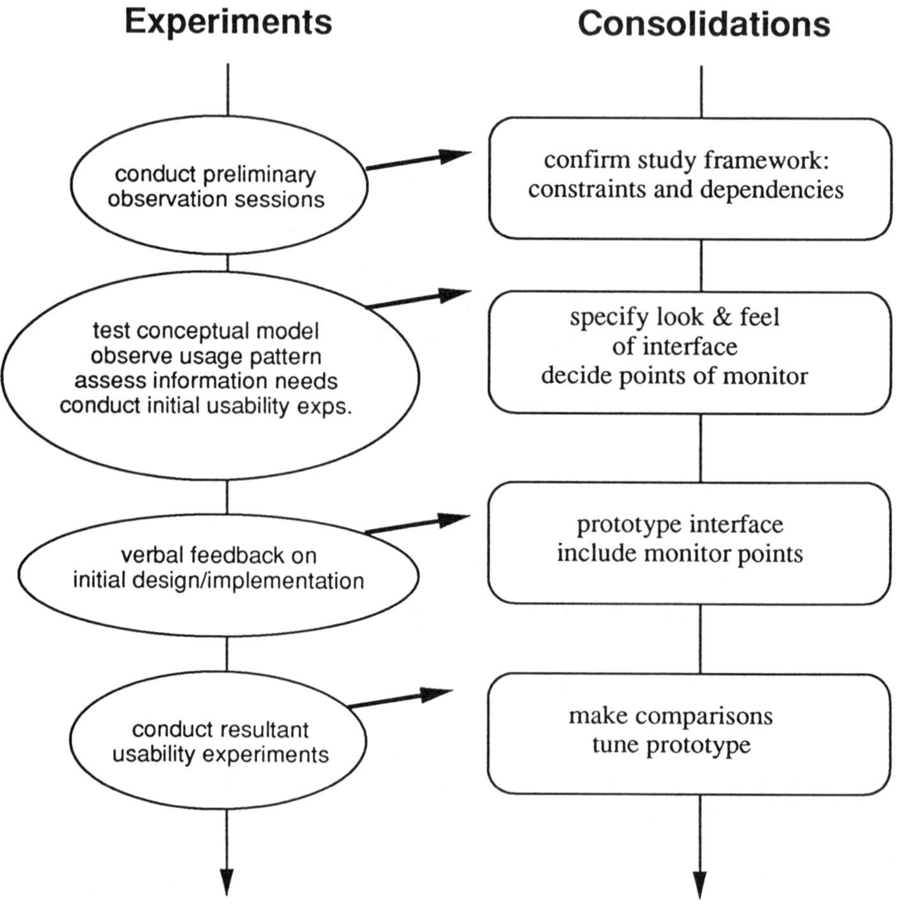

Figure 3.1 - Threads of iterative development

3.3 PROTOTYPING

3.3.1 Alternative Approaches to Prototyping

Prototyping and subsequent evaluation, of various kinds and degrees of sophistication, should occur throughout the process of evolving a multimedia interface. Figure 3.1 gives an outline of the evaluative steps involved in this evolution.

A vital part of the iterative design process is to expose users to emerging ideas about possible realizations of the interface, and the sooner the better.

Rapid prototyping aims to avoid travelling too far down any one particular path without first making sure that the destination is where we want to be. Certainly, once we are committed to an implementation, we want if at all possible not to make major changes. It is far better to give prospective users as realistic an idea as possible of where the design is leading so that feedback can be obtained, through one means or another, to steer the design activity.

The alternatives for rapid prototyping represent increasingly expensive and committed (and, hence, chronologically sequential) approaches to gaining usability feedback. At its simplest, prototyping may involve nothing more than the production of paper mockups, accompanied by a rough script of the course of interactions with the (as yet imaginary) interface. A step further on, detailed scenarios or story boards provide detailed runs through a range of interactions, on the basis of which the target users can get a good idea of the prospective interface, and provide their feedback through discussion or by filling out questionnaires.

Similar in concept, but even more realistic, video prototypes (Vertelney, 1989) create the impression that the interface already exists, since actors can be seen interacting with the system on video. However, video prototypes are actually fakes, since the apparent functionality of the application does not yet exist. The danger with video prototypes is that designers may be tempted to exaggerate the capabilities of the future interface, so that the video becomes more of an advertizement for a possible future than an evaluative tool for a realistic design. The main limitation with all of these methods is that, since the interface does not exist, the prospective users cannot actually interact with them. Mind experiments can only take one so far; many unexpected problems and insights will result from actual, spontaneous, behaviour with the interface.

Sometimes parts of an interface can be readily produced for evaluation, typically the visual and auditory *displays* and *forms*, but other aspects cannot be produced without major effort, for example the dialogue components that produce *actions* and *effects*. With the so-called 'Wizard of Oz' technique (e.g. Diaper, 1986), the intelligence underlying the dialogue components of the interface are simulated by the use of the same simple subterfuge employed by the chess-playing automaton demonstrated by von Kempelen at the end of the 18th century: a hidden human working behind the scenes as the dialogue controller and intelligence of the system. This approach has most often been applied to test out database query systems and expert systems, and is probably less suitable for multimedia interface design where the emphasis is on immediate flexible response through parallel media channels rather than relatively intelligent, turn-taking interactions through a single channel.

Ideally, realistic implementations can be produced and modified rapidly to allow genuine evaluation of designs to take place. The development of rapid prototyping tools is making a major impact on the process of designing multimedia interfaces (see section 3.5.2 below). There are, however, times when the temptation to develop a prototype should be resisted. These include: when the application is so ill-defined that little or no task analysis can be carried out, when essential elements of proposed interactions cannot be simulated, when the users have not been identified, and when expectations of users or their (or the designers) managers are unrealistic.

3.3.2 Rapid Prototyping Tools

The term user interface management system (UIMS) describes a discrete software module or set of modules that minimizes the amount of direct programming needed to specify interface and dialogue features of an application. The main justification for UIMSs is thus to eliminate some of the time-consuming and laborious low-level programming work needed for UI specification, especially for graphical display.

Hayes and Szekely(1983) outline additional advantages. Because UIMSs typically employ abstractions of interface behaviour, specifications are relatively concise. A fully fledged UIMS will also have the capability for running the dialogue and its interactions with the application, thus providing a prototyping environment. The claimed ease of specification means that saved effort can be directed to providing enhanced features such as intelligent help and good error correction. Human factors specialists, sometimes referred to as 'dialogue authors' (Hartson and Johnson, 1983), can apply expertise to design and experiment with new interfaces independently from the applications programming.

Interfaces developed using UIMSs will tend to be more consistent, thus increasing learnability and ease of use. On the other hand, different specifications can be developed for the same application, so that comparisons between candidate designs can be made, perhaps testing different input/output devices or catering for varying skill levels and preferences. The possibilities for rapid prototyping and iterative development (Schulert *et al.*, 1985) are perhaps the most valuable features of such systems.

Figure 3.2 illustrates one current way of conceptualizing a UIMS as a set of reconfigurable UI code modules that can be reused with different applications (Cardwell, 1987). Included in the system is a set of tools for producing specifications that define how modules will be realized for particular applications.

The presentation component is responsible for the external presentation of the UI. It is the only component the user communicates with, it generates the images that actually appear on the screen, and reads the input devices, converting raw data into a higher level form. In most current systems, a textual programming language is used to specify interface ideas.

The dialogue control component defines and structures the dialogue between the user and the application. It interprets input from the presentation and sends this information to the application. Information from the application may be restructured and sent to the presentation component. It also has access to operating system messages and help routines. The most common notations for dialogue control specification are grammars (Olsen and Dempsey, 1983; Reisner, 1981; Ronnquist, 1984), transition networks (Jacob, 1985; Wasserman and Shewmake, 1985), or both (Edmonds and Guest, 1984).

The application component defines the semantics of the application. It has knowledge of data structures in the application, procedures that affect dialogue control, and the constraints placed on the user by the application. Little is currently known about how to design a uniform application interface, however. Fisher and Joy (1987) describe interesting exploratory work in this area.

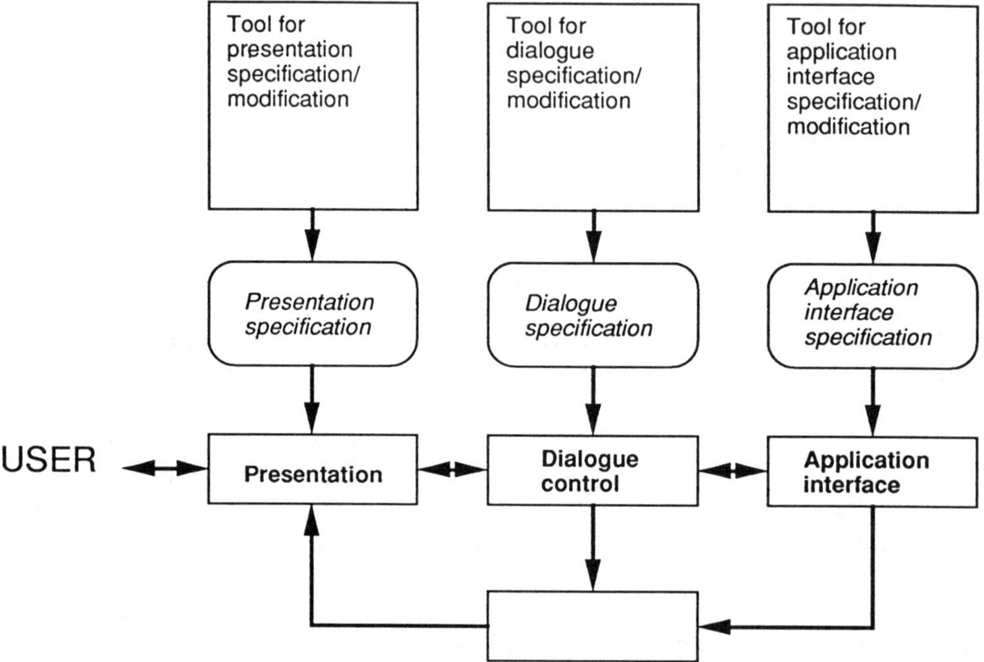

Figure 3.2 - UIMS architecture

The dream of rapid, easy specification of good UIs to complex systems is an
attractive one. Unfortunately, the promises have not been fulfilled. The main
shortcomings of UIMSs, which have led to their being relatively little used as yet,
are: difficulty of use, limitations in functionality, and lack of portability (Lowgren,
1988). A major reason for the difficulty of use with many UIMSs is the lack of
convenient notations. Transition networks and grammars were a natural way of
specifying simple interaction styles, such as command languages, form filling, and

menus; they are much less appropriate for graphical, direct manipulation interfaces. The designer must be a specialist in the interface and dialogue notations (which are often as complex as a programming language) and, even then, will find it difficult to visualize the results of the specification during its construction.

Another problem with the specification of direct manipulation interfaces is the need for immediate semantic feedback. If an object representing a file is 'dragged' over the 'trashcan', for example, the representation of the can must change its appearance immediately. However, the multi-module structure of many UIMSs may not permit sufficiently fast response to presentation events that depend on the semantics of the application layer.

From a multimedia perspective, current UIMSs do not have sufficient flexibility or scope to handle a range of different media. They cannot be used for specifying state-of-the-art interfaces. For these reasons, UIMSs have not yet been widely accepted by UI designers.

3.3.3 New Developments and Trends

3.3.3.1 Interface Specification

New ways for designers to specify the features of multimedia UIs are being developed, to overcome the problems of hard to use notations, limited flexibility, and the difficulty of visualizing results. If UIMSs are ever to be widely used by UI designers, they must themselves provide convenient interfaces for their users, i.e. the UI designers. Direct manipulation techniques, applied at the designer's interface, provide a visual programming environment that allows different versions of (essentially graphical) interface designs to be explored (e.g. Singh and Green, 1988). Other variations of this approach include 'programming by example' and 'programming by rehearsal'.

Peridot (Myers, 1987a) allows the designer to demonstrate how the input devices should be handled by drawing the display and providing examples of the way the interface should perform. Once sample values have been provided, the system is able to generalize about performance and create the appropriate code. Peridot (Programming by Example for Real-time Interface Design Obviating Typing) is aimed predominantly at rapid design, implementation and modification of WIMP interfaces at the level of widget creation.

Druid (Demonstrational Rapid User Interface Development), an advanced UIMS currently under development (Singh, 1991; Singh *et al.*, 1990) takes the demonstrational model a stage further. Druid assumes the basic widgets and allows layouts to be created by direct manipulation, aided by system inferences about the way the designer is trying to design the presentation. Demonstration is used to specify the behavioural component of an interface. This is more natural and convenient than the use of special purpose specification languages or graphical notations. The designer turns on a recorder and then runs through the sequence of interaction to be specified. The recorder can be paused and restarted until all the necessary actions for a particular function have been captured. From this recording, Druid automatically produces the necessary code to implement the demonstrated behaviour patterns (see Figure 3.3).

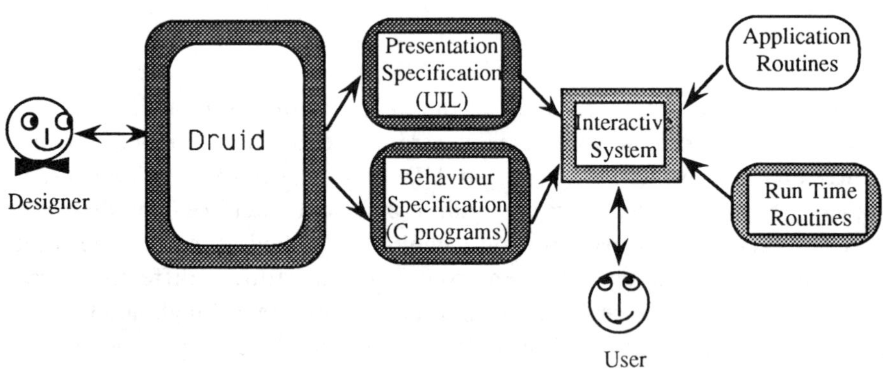

Figure 3.3 - The Druid UIMS

3.3.3.2 Construction Kits

The simpler a UIMS is to use, the more limited is the range of interfaces it can generate. Very general purpose UIMSs cannot deal conveniently with specialized applications. Recognition of this trade-off has led to the recent development of specialized construction kits for particular application domains (Fischer and Lemke, 1988). Another major reason for this trend is the need to facilitate the creation of interfaces for specific task needs. Fischer and Lemke refer to this as 'Human Problem-Domain Communication'. They define a construction kit as a set of building blocks that models a problem domain. Key features of this approach are the appropriateness of the blocks to a given type of task, and the easy restructuring of the blocks to suit the user's needs (Winograd, 1979).

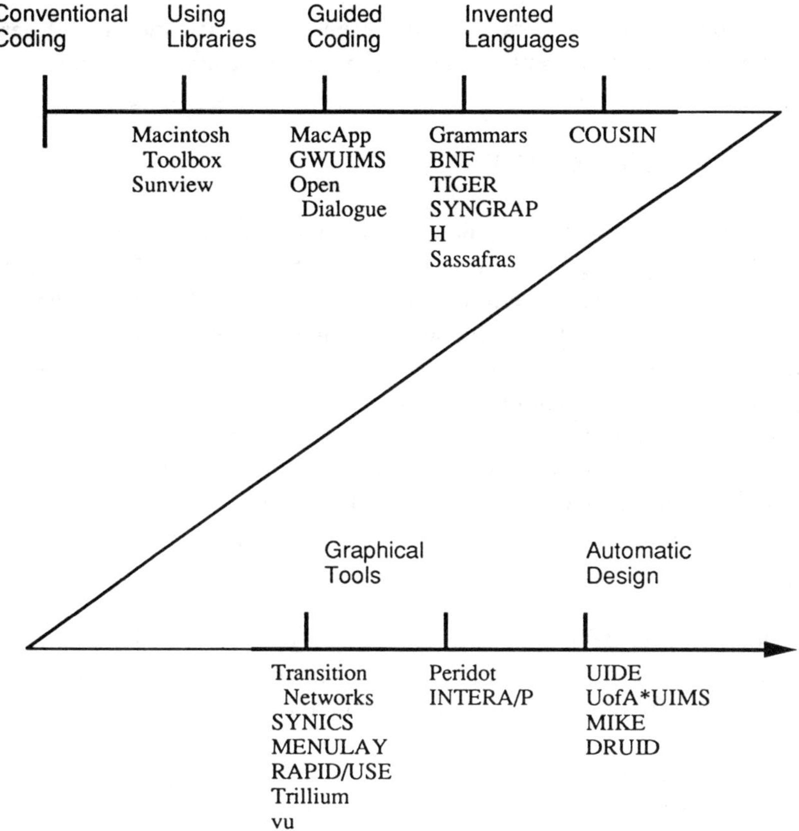

Figure 3.4 - Classification of UI design tools

3.3.3.3 Incorporating Knowledge

Once a construction kit becomes rich enough to meet the design needs of a complex task domain, ease of use again becomes a problem. Fischer and Lemke (1988) suggest that, in addition to adequate construction components, "Tools are needed to aid in making design decisions, carry out low-level details, analyse or criticize intermediate versions, and visualize their structure. These tools incorporate knowledge that goes beyond what went into the design of individual components. Specifically, they have additional domain knowledge to aid in the design of reasonable artifacts" (p. 199). They refer to these knowledgeable toolkits as design environments. The idea of incorporating UI design knowledge within a general purpose UIMS has also been explored (e.g. Foley *et al.*, 1988).

Figure 3.4 (adapted from Myers, 1987b) presents a classification of UI design tools along a continuum from conventional coding to automatic interface design.

3.4 SOME DESIGN OPTIONS

There has been an emergence of new forms of interaction over the last couple of decades, initially quite gradual, but now breathtakingly rapid. The most obvious manifestation is in the basic style of human-computer dialogues. In the early days, interaction via command language, where sequences of special tokens had to be learned to carry out almost any useful actions, was all that was available. Command languages are still popular with expert users, who can interact efficiently and flexibly on the basis of their sophisticated knowledge of the system and the language, and create their own 'macros' for complex sequences of instructions, thus exercising a very high level of initiative. For lots of tasks and for less experienced users, however, command languages are inappropriate, largely because of their poor error handling, and the need for substantial training and memorization.

Menu selection was developed as a technique of reducing both keystrokes and errors, at the same time as minimizing the need for learning. For some situations, selection of items from a menu of available functions is entirely appropriate: choosing from a list of fonts in a word processing application, for example. But if the number of alternatives becomes too large, there is a tendency for the user to be confronted with many menu choices. This slows down frequent users enormously, and large amounts of screen space are needed, with a rapid display rate between menus.

Form filling was aimed principally at applications where many examples of fairly small, well-structured data sets are to be entered repeatedly, such as in some business accounts applications. As with menus, little training is needed, data entry is simple, and on-line assistance can be easily provided. Again, a large amount of screen space is used, but the speed of the interaction is less pedestrian than with menus.

In recent years, there have been two main developments that have significantly altered the nature of human-computer exchanges: natural language processing and direct manipulation interfaces.

The idea of users being able to 'talk to' the system in their own language has an obvious appeal. In practice the picture is less ideal (Rich, 1984). Natural languages, unlike artificial ones, are highly ambiguous, redundant, context-dependent, and idiosyncratic to individuals. Processing natural language is thus difficult, error-prone, and expensive. Also, a natural language interface can be seen as promising too much: the intelligence of the system as a whole may not live up to the expectation the user builds up from the style of interaction. The universe to which natural language applies uniquely well will always be larger than the coverage of the system, no matter how good the syntactic processing, so that context and dialogue knowledge must also be developed. In general, a large number of keystrokes will be needed, unless speech is the basis of interaction (which has its own problems). But natural language is well suited to many situations, such as consulting expert knowledge sources, negotiating the details of a user's informational needs, and retrieving textual information flexibly from large databases.

The most revolutionary change to interfaces, a move away from viewing interaction as some kind of sequential dialogue between user and system, was the development of techniques for direct on-screen manipulation of objects representing actions and entities within the system. With a WIMP interface (windows, icons, menus, pointing), users with little or no experience can carry out basic operations, such as filing, deleting and copying, without error and without having to learn any arcane language or procedures. Exploration is encouraged, so that users quickly pick up additional skills. This engenders a feeling of confidence which in part explains the great popularity of WIMP systems. A further aspect of the appeal is the sheer excitement of directly interacting with a consistent, but artificial reality (Hutchins *et al.*, 1986).

Multimedia interaction is another, even more revolutionary, step forward in the way humans interact with computers. No existing style is ideal for all purposes, and there are some types of operation, such as detailed data entry, for which direct manipulation can be highly laborious. The technique also requires good quality graphics and the ability to readily describe system functions and data structures as iconic symbols. Recent developments in multimedia have pointed to the need for integrative styles of interaction, combining some features from the direct manipulation situation while retaining the feeling of communication with an intermediary.

There is evidence that providing users with a clear metaphorical model, as compared to giving procedural instructions, to carry out a task, leads to improved efficiency and memorability (Borgman, 1986a; Payne, 1987). I consider the use of analogy for multimedia interaction design in some detail in Chapter 5.

Chapter 4

Hypermedia: Current Concerns, Future Directions

with Mark H Chignell

"He looked into the water and saw that it was made up of a thousand thousand thousand and one different currents, each one a different colour, weaving in and out of one another like a liquid tapestry of breathtaking complexity; and Iff explained that these were the Streams of Story, that each coloured strand represented and contained a single tale. Different parts of the Ocean contained different sorts of stories, and as all the stories that had ever been told and many that were still in the process of being invented could be found there, the Ocean of the Streams of Story was in fact the biggest library in the universe. And because the stories were held here in fluid form, they retained the ability to change, to become new versions of themselves, to join up with other stories and so become yet other stories; so that unlike a library of books, the Ocean of the Streams of Story was much more than a storeroom of yarns. It was dead but alive.

'And if you are very, very careful, or very, very highly skilled, you can dip a cup into the Ocean,' Iff told Haroun, 'like so', and here he produced a little golden cup from another of his waistcoat pockets, 'and you can fill it with water from a single, pure Stream of Story, like so', as he did precisely that, 'and then you can offer it to a young fellow who's feeling blue, so that the magic of the story can restore his spirits. Go on now; knock it back, have a swig, do yourself a favour,' Iff concluded. 'Guaranteed to make you feel A-number-one.'

Haroun, without saying a word, took the golden cup and drank."

- from *Haroun and the Sea of Stories* by Salman Rushdie, pp71-2,
   published by Granta Books, London, 1990.

4.1 INTRODUCTION: INTERFACE DESIGN FOR HYPERMEDIA

Our purpose in this chapter is to outline what we see as the main research issues that must be addressed to make the future exploitation of hypermedia systems a success. We begin by considering what is already known about the usability of hypermedia. Some issues arise from general considerations of interface design for information systems. We consider these first and then review aspects of usability that are more specifically related to hypermedia itself.

4.1.1 Issues from Conventional Interface Design

The issues that affect the usability of hypermedia often reflect those that already exist in conventional user interfaces. For instance, the problem of disorientation (getting lost in spaghetti) that seems particularly important in large associative information networks also exists in a large menu structure consisting of many levels, and many items within the menus at each level. Each interface that is designed has to balance the need to make a large amount of information available through multiple access routes with the need to maintain the orientation of users so that they know where they are and what can be done within the current context. Thus interface designers are routinely faced with questions such as: how can users find their way around the system, get back to where they want to be, not fail to visit relevant areas; without sacrificing the freedom to explore, make new connections, and take novel routes?

Similarly, the problems of locating particular information within a hypermedia system are inherently part of a general model of information seeking behaviour (see Chapter 6). Hypermedia simply further encourages alternative structuring principles. Hypermedia neither creates a new type of information retrieval problem, nor does it solve existing problems. It encourages a larger variety of information seeking activities than is conventionally available, each of which has an associated set of interface design challenges.

Even prior to the advent of hypermedia systems, the role of structure in good interface design was unclear. For instance, Shneiderman (1987a, Chapter 3) cites a study by Tombaugh and McEwen (1982) that compared retrieval performance on videotex systems using tree-structure versus alphabetic directories. They found no significant differences in mean search time, number of keypresses, or number of menus accessed between the two conditions. In addition, subjective evaluations did not favour one method over the other, but when one method required more pages for a specific question, the preference was for the shorter method. In terms of usability it seems that how the user perceives interface structure is at least as important as what structures are actually used (Mantei, 1982).

If hypermedia interfaces do not resolve existing issues of how to handle structure, neither do they imply solutions to fundamental concerns about the style of interaction to use when expressing queries, initiating actions, and so on. It has generally been assumed that a direct manipulation (Shneiderman, 1987a, Chapter 5; Hutchins *et al.*, 1986) style of interaction should be used for hypermedia, but there is little research to support this intuition. Interactions using menu selections and command languages have not, for most users, been superseded by direct manipulation in conventional interfaces. While hypermedia seems to encourage the types of graphical presentation that are typical of direct manipulation, possible roles for menu selection and command languages should not be overlooked.

Experience with conventional interfaces also has implications for attempts to develop standardized hypermedia. Lack of standards for hypertext has been cited as a current problem (e.g., Parsaye *et al.*, 1989; p. 269), yet why should standards for hypermedia be any easier to achieve than standards for interface design in general? Appropriate design of interfaces appears to depend at least partially on the type of task being carried out. For instance, a spreadsheet model works well for a financial analysis program, but not for word processing.

As long as hypermedia systems are conceived of as being used in a small range of tasks (i.e., information seeking within associative structures) a quest for standardization might seem reasonable, but why should hypermedia be limited simply to basic information retrieval? Already, hypermedia has been used to implement design aiding systems (Conklin and Begeman, 1987), cooperative authoring systems (Trigg and Irish, 1987), and computer-based instructional systems (e.g., Chignell and Lacy, 1988). Thus, as the tasks to which hypermedia may be applied multiply, the quest for standardization in hypermedia interfaces becomes more problematic. It is not yet clear how structural decisions about hypermedia implementation will affect user performance in different tasks. For instance, should a hypermedia ideas tool have the same sort of structure as a hypermedia anatomy-teaching system? How can task-relevant differences in hypermedia be characterized?

It is interesting to note that people seem to expect more of hypermedia systems than they do of conventional interfaces. Most existing user interfaces have very little scope for being tailored to meet specific user needs, yet such tailorability seems to be obligatory in the "brave new world" of hypermedia.

In our view, generic hypermedia is not very well suited to any particular task. Thus it is an open question as to how hypermedia should be configured for the needs of particular tasks and how it should be tailored to meet the needs of users and extended functionalities that they may require.

4.1.2   Empirical Studies of Hypermedia Usability

Several major interface and design issues have been identified from existing hypermedia research. Many of these issues are described in Halasz (1988). So far, however, relatively little detailed empirical research has been carried out of hypermedia in realistic use to back this up. Field studies provide one approach to achieving greater 'ecological validity'. For instance, Hardman (1989) examined the usability of a hypertext system but, unfortunately, used artificially created situations and interviews. Nielsen and Lyngbaek (1989) also failed to achieve the necessary realism of use. Such methods make statistical analysis and generalization problematic, although they do give hints on the usefulness of certain types of structure and linking strategies. The field studies currently available make it difficult to draw specific conclusions about features of hypermedia systems. In general, studies that have explicitly investigated the effects of different independent variables seem to be more informative than studies that seek to evaluate the overall effectiveness of a hypermedia application. Examples of the former type of study include Egan *et al.* (1989), Hammond and Allinson (1987, 1988), Marchionini and Shneiderman (1988), McKnight *et al.* (1989), Simpson and McKnight (1989), Weyer (1982), and Wright and Lickorish (1989). This work is briefly reviewed below, followed by an overview of some major issues specific to the design of hypermedia systems.

In an early study, Weyer (1982) pointed to the negative side of providing sophisticated navigational tools; users probably will not use them much unless they have extensive training. Based on their previous experience, users are rather likely to interact with new systems in ways that, to the system designers, are extremely inefficient. This may in part account for users' continued preference for more traditional forms of information organization in some situations.

Hammond and Allinson (1987) compared users' recognition for system facilities such as reading lists and glossaries. Half of the facilities they tested were actually present in the system which users had encountered, half were not; additionally, half of each of these sets could be clearly mapped onto the overall metaphor of the system, while the other half could not. They found that facilities that were suggested by the metaphor but were actually absent were often, and confidently, judged to be present. Surprisingly, facilities within the metaphor were less well recognized than those outside the metaphor, perhaps because the latter were much more frequently used. These findings have important implications for the successful use of analogy in hypermedia interface design (see Chapter 5).

In a later study, the same authors (Hammond and Allinson, 1988) assessed how different information retrieval facilities are utilized for various information seeking tasks, as indicated by subjects' judgements of usage. For example, subjects judged that "browsing" was most often carried out via a map, whereas they thought that "information search" had mostly used an index. Though the evidence is not strong, the principle that different facilities are needed for different tasks is clearly demonstrated. Marchionini and Shneiderman (1988) see browsing as an exploratory information-seeking strategy that depends on serendipity for success. As such, success or otherwise could be seen as depending on chance. There is actually a general problem with evidence in relation to browsing tools, arising from the difficulty of specifying adequate criteria for success that can be tested in a rigorous way.

A few studies have compared information retrieval with hypertext versus more traditional linear presentation. McKnight *et al.* (1989), for example, presented the same material in two hypertext formats, as a word processor document, and on paper. Subjects had to answer 12 questions which, the authors claim, would "ensure that a range of information retrieval strategies were employed to answer them and that the questions did not unduly favour any one medium". No differences were found in task completion time, but subjects answered more accurately with linear formats than with hypertext. Vastly more time was spent viewing the contents and index for the latter formats than with linear presentation. Subjects spent surprisingly little time following hypertext links, but a great deal of time jumping back and forth between text and indices. Scanning the text in a linear manner appeared to be a much more effective strategy than this. This finding is compatible with that of Monk *et al.* (1988, see 2.2). Egan *et al.* (1989), on the other hand, found that students using "Superbook" were more successful at answering search questions, writing 'open-book' essays, and recalling incidental information, than those using a conventional text version of the same material. This is attributable to the tools provided, such as sophisticated mediated information retrieval facilities and a 'fisheye viewer' which aided navigation by the user.

Further light is shed on the issues of navigational tool use by Wright and Lickorish (1989). Their experiment had users answering questions by consulting hypertext information accessed by two different navigation systems. One involved jumping to and from an index, while the other permitted direct jumps to other places in the information base.

Readers' preferences depended on the way the information was structured and the task they were performing. For a book-like hypertext, with modular information structure, navigation via an index was preferred. But with a less book-like text, with a symmetrically hierarchical structure, 'page navigation' was preferred and gave better performance on some types of questions. The authors point out that what constitutes a successful design for a hypertext depends both on the inherent structure of the material and the tasks that users will wish to carry out. This points to the importance of providing alternative methods of navigation.

Simpson and McKnight (1989) found, not surprisingly, that a hierarchically structured contents list produced more efficient navigational behaviour than did an alphabetic index. Imposing structure is not always advantageous, however. Heppe *et al.* (1985), for example, point out the dangers of false hierarchies which do not match informational requirements for more than the very first user encounters with the system. Early decisions by users can easily become frozen in a structure that does not match their needs.

4.1.3   Summary of Design Issues Specific to Hypermedia Systems

Although the available behavioural evidence is somewhat thin, and far from unequivocal, common themes do emerge both from this and from other non-empirical work. It seems safe to conclude that navigation, where the user alone is responsible for finding his way around a complex undefined structure, will rarely if ever be enough for efficient access to the information contained in a large hypermedia system. What is currently unclear is how to reduce the cognitive load this responsibility places on the user, without sacrificing the freedom of exploration that is such an attractive feature of hypermedia.

Hierarchical organization of information is an obvious direction to move in, but it is potentially counter-productive to impose or fix this at too early a stage. The provision of easy revision facilities is one way around this problem. Ideally, it should be possible to reorganize material easily in new ways implying new hierarchies.

Without this, one of the principal benefits of hypermedia - flexible handling of an information base - has been lost. A necessary part of this flexibility is the facility to file things under several categories, re-arrange filing schemes easily, or access different views (embodying different categorization hierarchies) of the same information.

Sophisticated search facilities are essential to support complex queries. Users can often describe what they are looking for, even though they cannot find it themselves through navigation. Browsing and querying need to be harmoniously combined, so that users can browse then query, and vice versa. We have suggested elsewhere (Waterworth and Chignell, 1989b) that these activities are best regarded as points on a continuum rather than diversely discrete entities. What this will involve in practice is an intriguing question for future usability research (see section 4.2 below for further discussion on this point).

It is clear that the structural model, and associated methods for creating and using links, need to be sophisticated enough to support task requirements, but simple structural and interaction models may have advantages for collaborative authoring, largely because of their ease of understanding and mutual consistency of use (Yoder *et al.*, 1989). On the other hand, this work also suggests that oversimplification may be dangerous in some situations, as when the distinction between merely 'quitting' and 'quitting and saving' is lost. Visualization of information and structure, and extensibility of the structural and interaction models are also key issues for hypermedia, although the available research literature offers few insights into how they should be addressed.

The most important message from the available literature is that task needs must be taken more into account through, at least, easy tailorability. Users typically try to make allowances for the system's idiosyncrasies to meet their task needs. This gives them a great deal of extra work to do. Providing alternative structures, or views, may often be needed; for example when clearly different classes of users require access to the same hyperbase, or when users graduate through a series of skill levels (in computer-aided learning applications, for example). An empirical approach to task-adaptive design is needed, particularly for special purpose systems. In existing work, special-purpose systems have attempted to meet task needs, although the approaches have not been tested adequately against alternatives.

4.2 DIRECTIONS FOR FUTURE RESEARCH

In the last section we described several of the usability issues relevant to hypermedia. We also reviewed some of the relatively few studies that have so far been published. In this section, we outline possible approaches to these and other usability issues, and how they might be adapted to the special problems of hypermedia. We conclude the section with an outline of the fundamental user- and use-related questions that future hypermedia research must address.

4.2.1 Approaches to Usability

So far, hypermedia design has largely been ad hoc and the value, or otherwise, of incorporating various user-related features remains untested, except in a few exceptional cases (see section 4.1.2). The method of iterative design and test, which has widely been accepted as necessary to the development of highly usable interface designs, has not yet been widely applied to hypermedia systems. As we saw in the first section (4.1.1), it is also the case that existing knowledge of interface design issues, largely from human factors studies of applications other than hypermedia, has not been incorporated into the design process to any great extent. This may be partly due to the fact that hypermedia tends to break down traditional distinctions between information systems and their interfaces.

Previously, structure has tended to be embedded in the information system, while the interface has handled the process of navigation. However, hypermedia serves simultaneously as a structuring principle and as a navigational interface. Thus hypermedia provides a much more direct interface to information than is usually possible.

Seen from the perspective of the interface, hypermedia plays multiple roles:

>   (i) a conceptual structure that may be used to navigate amongst information,
>
>   (ii) a self generating menu system (this is akin to the notion of embedded menus championed by Shneiderman, 1987b),
>
>   (iii) a bridge between heterogeneous information structures (different media, database environments, text environments, etc.), and
>
>   (iv) a structural (often spatial) metaphor.

The intimate connection between hypermedia and the user interface means that hypermedia design and implementation has as much to do with interface design as it has to do with information storage. Thus the selection of information to be included in the system, the linking of information, and the visualization of information must all be viewed in the context of the navigation processes (and metaphors) available in the interface. Once we recognize the similarity between hypermedia design and interface design it then becomes possible to apply the concepts and techniques developed by human factors and other researchers to the enhancement of hypermedia.

In analyzing possible approaches to hypermedia usability we will consider three main orientations for incorporating a consideration of user characteristics and needs into the process of design. These are the empirical and the anthropometric research perspectives (see Eberts, 1987), the latter including recent work on conversational interaction, and visualization and its possible roles in future implementations.

4.2.2 The Empirical Approach

Empirical studies have traditionally addressed such issues as the relative merits of the mouse as an input device, the effectiveness of different menu design strategies, and the legibilities of different fonts and displays. The results of many of these studies can be applied directly to the design of hypermedia interfaces.

For instance, we might expect that the use of a mouse or other pointing device is likely to be as valid in hypermedia usage as it is in many computing applications. Card *et al.* (1978) compared the time taken for well-practiced subjects to select target words, from various positions around the screen, using either a mouse, arrow keys, a joystick, or special purpose text keys. In general, the mouse was quickest and the arrow keys slowest, except for very short selection distances, when the reverse was true. However, Ewing *et al.*(1986) found that performance with a mouse was consistently slower than with arrow keys when the task was to follow a path of embedded menus through an interactive encyclopaedia system (TIES). This diversity in findings points to the need for caution in applying previous results to new, potentially very different, interactive situations.

A great strength of appropriate empirical experimentation is the exposure of existing assumptions to practical evaluation. It is often claimed, for example, that the non-linearity of hypertext is especially well suited to effective browsing. But a study by Monk *et al.* (1988) illustrates that, in some circumstances at least, a scrolling browser is preferable to a hypertext browser. Not surprisingly, performance with the hypertext browser was significantly improved when an overview map of the information structure was provided. The authors make the important point that "finding your way about a hypertext structure may distract from the primary task" (Monk *et al.*, 1988, p. 433).

It is clear that future facilities for navigational and computer-mediated information retrieval will need to be subjected to detailed empirical testing. Some of the relatively few studies that have already addressed information retrieval issues connected with the use of hypermedia systems of different types were reviewed earlier in section 4.1. Many more such studies will be needed. In deciding what tools are appropriate for information seeking, within each specific interactive environment, particularly important factors will be the characteristics of the tasks users are attempting to carry out, and the nature of the information base with which they are working. Our clarification of the three major dimensions of information retrieval (see Chapter 6) is intended as a first step towards a disciplined approach to testing these usability factors.

A recent study by Monk (1989) illustrates the potential value of identifying the types of information seeking behaviour in which users are engaged. He distinguished between the situation where users wish to reach a known location to retrieve information on a particular topic, and the situation where the user does not know precisely where the information he is seeking might be located. He refers to these two cases as directed navigation and exploratory navigation, respectively. From this he is able to suggest an approach to browser design that should improve the ease with which tasks requiring directed navigation can be carried out. We need to study how information can best be structured for different tasks, and how different structures can best be conveyed to users and navigated by them.

Empirical studies are also likely to be particularly relevant to the successful adoption of new input and output techniques. Studies of users' perceptions of new visual representations of information structure, such as automated icons and 3-D spatial metaphors (Fairchild *et al.*, 1988; 1989), are likely to be important, along with detailed evaluations of the input techniques to be used during navigation of complex information structures. Examples of these new devices are the head-mounted display for 3-D graphics output, the Dataglove, for manipulating objects within three dimensions, and the Joystring, which provides appropriate force-feedback in response to users' physical movements (see Foley, 1987). The emergence and integration of devices such as these will involve a considerable amount of new empirical testing, along with careful interpretation of existing findings.

4.2.3 The Anthropomorphic Approach

The anthropomorphic approach looks to the world of human-human communication for inspiration about the nature of human-computer communication and interaction. Aspects of human-human communication that researchers have sought to transfer to human-computer communication include such concepts as partnership (Press, 1971), gracefulness (Hayes and Reddy, 1983), and transparency (Fitter, 1979).

The anthropomorphic approach generally sets standards for the type of interaction that should occur without necessarily providing the technology for achieving those standards. For instance, Ochsman and Chapanis (1974) found that in observing problem solving performance, problems were solved more efficiently through human-human interaction when voice was one of the communication channels used. However, the anthropomorphic approach can also show cases where extensive applications of sophisticated technologies may be unnecessary. For instance, Kelly and Chapanis (1977) used human-human communication as a model for determining the size of vocabulary needed to achieve satisfactory communication between human and computer when solving a problem. They found little deficit in problem solving performance when the vocabulary was restricted to 300 words as compared with an unrestricted vocabulary, suggesting that voice recognition of 300 words may be adequate for some HCI tasks.

Other studies have shown that the pursuit of naturalness for its own sake may not always be productive. For instance, Scapin (1981) compared command names that were "natural" with computer-oriented command names. In a free-recall memory task novices could more easily recall the functions of the command names that were computer-oriented. But as Eberts (1987) pointed out, this advantage may be due to the fact that the computer-oriented terms suffered less interference from usage in non-computer contexts.

4.2.3.1 Conversational Interaction

The idea of making human-computer dialogue designs in some way analogous to human-human conversation is becoming increasingly popular (Taylor *et al.*, 1989). This has arisen because of two main considerations. Firstly, disappointment with the progress of natural language understanding techniques based on traditional linguistics has led to a re-examination of how people understand language, especially spoken language, in conversational contexts. Secondly, attempts to achieve more appropriate and flexible styles of interaction for information systems of various kinds have identified useful parallels with the loosely-structured patterns of human conversation. In some cases, these elements have combined into an integrated approach that sees the processes of a wide range of information exchanges as 'conversational' (Murray and Bevan, 1984; Winograd and Flores, 1986). A key feature of conversations is that not only turns but topics may be interleaved; that is, they make use of quite subtle conventions of communication to permit non-linearity of interaction (e.g. Edmondson, 1989). Conversational interaction can be contrasted with direct manipulation, which takes as its model not human-human communication but the human use of tools and other artifacts (Hutchins, 1989).

The value of conversational interaction, in terms of our model of information-seeking user activity, is most obviously seen in the context of mediated information retrieval. But another important application is the way in which the user may wish to negotiate a particular interface configuration, or may seek 'meta-information' about the ways in which information may be sought or the system may be configured.

One approach, adopted from the ethnomethodological school of sociology, is that of Conversational Analysis (e.g. Schegloff and Sacks, 1973). This involves sampling naturally occurring interactive behaviour and identifying regularly occurring patterns of interaction. This approach has been applied to speech-based interrogation of databases by telephone, to identify not only the words and phrases used and their likely ordering, but also the strategies used to carry out confirmation, correction and error recovery (Waterworth, 1989; Waterworth and Talbot, 1987).

As a result of the conversational approach, 'natural dialogue' (Taylor, 1989) is likely to become increasingly popular as an interactive technique for hypermedia, as with other large information systems. Natural dialogue, based on interpreting the language used in real information exchanges between people and, potentially, between users and systems, can be characterized in three important ways. Firstly, natural dialogue is not exclusively, or even necessarily, language-based; information in a variety of media and forms is naturally included. Secondly, the language used in natural dialogue is not well-formed. Thirdly, natural dialogue is always embedded in an interactive situation.

Recent work on natural dialogue shows considerable promise for various forms of information-seeking activities in hypermedia. In fact, relatively simple techniques, devoid of complex, context-independent knowledge about what is linguistically correct, can yield surprisingly successful results. Some of the key features of a "habitable" interface are described by Guindon (1988). Robustness, in dealing with loosely formed input, and rapid response time are vital. The interface must also be able to cover the sort of input users will naturally want to provide in a given interactive situation. This knowledge can be built up through users' real encounters with an evolving system, given a means of storing cases of situations, and of assembling a library of corresponding inputs and combinations of inputs. This is the approach taken by Whalen and Patrick (1989) in the design of their 'Conversational Hypertext' prototype. What has so far not been achieved is an integration of navigation and computer-mediated information retrieval involving both conversational and direct manipulation styles.

4.2.4   Visualizing Hypermedia

Hypermedia structures are constrained by the abilities of users to comprehend their structure. Visualization of structure is a method for increasing the amount of structural complexity that users can handle. Navigation tools are used to provide visualizations of hypermedia structure. Such tools, often referred to as browsers, range from the three-dimensional space provided in the SemNet project (Fairchild *et al.*, 1988) to tree structures that are used to show the hierarchical organization of nodes (Halasz *et al.*, 1987). Visualizations often consist of maps, or sets of visual cues that inform users about where they are relative to other information, and where they can move to given their current location. Methods for visualizing hypermedia may be classified as either spatial or non-spatial in nature.

Whilst we can expect considerable advantages from the use of visualization techniques, fundamental questions about how humans navigate around spatial structures have yet to be adequately addressed (Chignell, 1989). One of the major unresolved issues in hypermedia usage is how to provide visualization tools based on spatial models of information. This is intimately related to the use of metaphor at the hypermedia interface (see Chapter 5).

The various dimensions of information retrieval in hypermedia need to be integrated at the user interface (we cover this topic in detail in Chapter 6). The alternation between using search tools for information retrieval and then navigating hypermedia structure is, in terms of visualization, a bit like swimming underwater and then raising one's head to see where one has reached. But it does not necessarily follow that the search tool should be superimposed onto a spatial representation. Problems may arise through trying to do everything in the spatial domain. A conservative approach is to use spatial representation and graphics as context-sensitive tools rather than a complete and uniform representation for the set of information elements. On the other hand, the benefits from one integrated view of the hyperspace and available tools may outweigh the costs. These are issues for future experimentation.

Recently, there has been interest in the visualization of information objects themselves. This is the basis of the automated icon idea proposed by Fairchild *et al.* (1989). Automated icons could presumably be used to construct representations of information objects whose visual features provide cues to critical features of the objects being represented. Automated icons may then be embedded in both spatial and non-spatial visualizations of hypermedia.

Automated icons seem to raise some challenging computer graphics issues. Ideally, one should be able to build a knowledge base that controls the creation and animation of automated icons in different circumstances. One could then define an icon creation palette or library of objects, such as faces, books, etc. that can be generated by a set of rules operating on the representations of objects. For example, if the object is a person then use a face, if the person is a male above a certain age colour the face dark blue, and so on.

4.2.5   Using Hypermedia in the Future: key issues

The potential benefits and pitfalls of hypermedia flexibility mean that we need to think about structure, browsing and information retrieval in new ways. Many tasks do not fall exclusively into the domain of browsing or of targeted information retrieval (conventional database query) but instead involve some combination of the two. It is an open question as to whether present tendencies towards using indexes and reading large linear chunks of text will continue to persist as people learn to use hypermedia systems (see Barrett, 1988, p.xiii-xxv). There is little documentation on how people use hypermedia over a period of time, and almost no consideration at all of how people should be trained to use hypermedia systems given their unfamiliarity with it and their extensive background in older technologies.

This is not just a problem with hypermedia, but with electronic information in general. Systems designers have been raised in societies dominated by linear media such as books and television. These linear media have encouraged a relatively passive style of presentation. In order to exploit the potential of hypermedia as an interface to information technology the surprisingly passive nature of current hypermedia systems will have to give way to a more actively helpful approach. At present, hypermedia allows us to create vast networks of association, but does not help us interpret this network (Jones, 1987).

4.2.5.1 Relevance

What is missing most is a consideration of relevance in context, and also of importance (global relevance) considered across the network. Both should lead to an actively changing representation of structure. Thus users are no longer forced to accept the importance of topics as defined by the author for all readers, but may assign their own relevance or importance to information. This idea has been exploited previously in the development of relevance feedback within information retrieval systems (Salton and McGill, 1983).

Relevance is a vital factor in cognition and communication, and is conspicuous by its general absence in hypermedia. (Sperber and Wilson, 1986, provide an excellent account of the role of relevance in communication and cognition). The precise way in which relevance should be incorporated within hypermedia remains a challenge. In calculating which topics should be of relevance to 'guides' within their hypermedia application system, Salomon *et al.* (1989) developed a measure of relevance based on the co-occurrence of topical indexing terms in the guide and article indexing lists. Other approaches to relevance include the use of interest profiles, to determine relevance for different users, and the creation of contexts that define user interests at different points in a task.

4.2.5.2 Importance

While relevance may be defined by the user or the current context, importance represents a concept of salience that is less situation- or user-specific. Important topics may serve as landmarks that anchor the surrounding nodes within the hypermedia. One approach to determining importance or identifying landmarks is connectivity (Valdez *et al.*, 1988; Chignell, 1989). The basic idea of connectivity measures is that more important topics tend either to be connected to lots of other topics directly or are connected to other topics that are in turn well connected.

A fundamentally similar approach has been taken to the problems of identifying the most important parts of a text for the purpose of summarization (e.g. Hoey, 1983). At its simplest, each sentence in a block of text is regarded as a node, which becomes linked to other sentence nodes by the co-occurence of a word or a lexically related word (which could be done via morphological rules, and a thesaurus of word relations). The sentences with the most connections to other sentences are regarded as central in conveying the message contained within the text as a whole.

Taken a stage further, other characteristics, such as the presence of certain surface features such as subordinations, conjuncts, repetitions, and lexical signals, can provide additional information on supporting or contrasting sentences, logical sequence of an argument, and so on. This work provides a useful orientation for thinking about ways in which selected tours through a hyperbase can be configured, providing different degrees of detail while maintaining a certain amount of content- and media-related integrity.

There are also intriguing possibilities for the use of natural language processing for summarization of text contents of hyperbases and also for the enhancement of descriptive interaction. Well-known problems associated with information retrieval based on keywords, or Boolean combinations of keywords (e.g., Borgman, 1986b), motivate the use of what has been termed 'natural dialogue' (Taylor, 1989), most obviously as an alternative for descriptive computer-mediated querying (Waterworth and Chignell, 1989b).

A second approach to importance in hypermedia derives not from the structure of the hypermedia itself but from the pattern of usage. Such measures represent an interaction between hypermedia structure and user interests and reflect a composite of relevance and importance. Using a memory model approach (e.g. Jones, 1986), frequency or recency of use may be used to define relevance/importance. However, the process of differentially strengthening nodes or links based on usage is potentially dangerous in a system that is supposed to give user and system a shared context. The danger lies in the possibility that they may tend to forget the same things, with some items becoming irretrievable. However, forgetting could sometimes be a useful process for unwanted information, and it may be useful to create a distinction between short- and long-term memories in hypermedia, so that some information is readily available whereas other information can only be retrieved with more effort. The advantage of this approach is that the user's immediate workspace does not get cluttered up with unwanted information.

Ideally, one could have a self-configuring representation for browsing (and query) based on richness of connections and on past patterns of information retrieval, thus integrating structure and search in the interface representation.

4.2.5.3   Selective Views

We also need the notions of screens or filters for particular users and types of tasks. Weighting of relevance may be thought of as a mild filter that is put on information, but more generally information should be tailored to the needs of the user. However, here there will be a tradeoff between hiding information that the user probably does not want to know about and including enough information so that the educated guesses of the system do not end up excluding a topic that eventually turns out to be vital to the user.

The idea of screens and filters reflects the fact that for a single application there will be not one hypermedia network but many. For each user the functional network will consist of all the nodes that they could conceivably be interested in for the current context. This functional network (neighbourhood) would then inherit all the links from the global hypermedia system that connect pairs of nodes that also existed in the functional network. In addition to filtering nodes to arrive at functional networks we may also filter links to reduce the branching complexity within a hypermedia network. Thus the processes of link and node filtering may be combined to provide contextually tailored hypermedia systems.

In this chapter we have identified in some detail a number of vital areas of exploration for progress towards truly usable and adaptive hypermedia. It is important to remember that whatever features are provided in our interactive environments must be made intelligible to their users. Increasingly, familiarity with real-world objects and processes is being capitalized upon, through the use of analogy at the human-computer interface. In addition, systems need to provide user- and task-centred characteristics through dynamic structuring. We turn to these two topics in the following chapter.

Chapter 5

Analogy and Dynamism in Multimedia Design

"The greatest thing by far is to have a command of metaphor, ... To employ metaphors happily and effectively it is necessary to have an eye for resemblances."

Aristotle, *The Poetics*   (quoted by Gittens, 1986)

5.1   INTRODUCTION

One of the most effective, and currently popular, ways of making the features of complex computer-based systems more intelligible to those who work with them is through the use of analogy. In principle this is extremely simple: to improve ease of use and learning through similarities between the system features and the way other, more familiar, mechanisms or processes are already known to operate. By explicitly identifying a real-world analogy, by employing an interface 'metaphor', the characteristics which users would expect to be associated with the real-world object are implicitly transferred to the interface through which the user is interacting (see Carroll *et al.*, 1988).

5.2 METAPHORS IN INTERFACE DESIGN

There is a clear and seemingly irresistible trend to improve the adaptiveness of users' models of systems, and to increase compatibility with the designer's intended model, by incorporating metaphors within interface designs. Recent developments such as graphical bit-mapped displays combined with direct manipulation, on the one hand, and turn-taking conversational style interaction on the other, make the inclusion of some level of analogy in future interfaces inevitable. These two approaches represent the two underlying analogies on which all current metaphorical interfaces depend.

The object-handling tool-based style inherent in direct manipulation is so persuasive, and is becoming so pervasive, that many users do not think of it as an analogy to the real world, but as the actual reality of computer systems. The most common example of this type of interface that is generally recognized as metaphorical is the 'desktop'. Here, a more specific metaphor is built on top of the underlying real-world-object analogy. Similarly, conversational interfaces rely on regarding HCI as analogous to human-human communication. On top of this basic idea a more specialized metaphor, say an expert tour guide, can be developed. Conversational-type metaphors are somewhat less immediately assimilated as reality than are direct manipulation approaches, simply because we are less successful at developing surrogate people than we are at producing realistic representations of the process of manipulating objects.

A further development of the desktop theme, aimed at avoiding the problems of switching between different activities on the same workstation (while avoiding a cluttered desktop), is that of Rooms (Card and Henderson, 1987). The basic idea is to use different 'rooms' for different tasks (mail, control office, debate, etc.), enhanced with metaphor-consistent features such as Room redecoration, Doors and Back Doors, suites of Rooms, and pockets for carrying items from Room to Room. This illustrates how metaphors may evolve from simple, underlying, and general styles of interaction, to highly specialized, elaborate, and more limited simulations for very particular application purposes.

The rationale of designing a computer system in terms of one or more metaphors is, of course, that this capitalizes on the user's world knowledge to help him understand the way in which the system works. If an interface display looks and works like a desktop, for example, the user will already know how to deal with documents and other items he finds there. So need for learning is minimized through predictability in terms of how real world objects behave. Or so the story goes. Nelson (1990) takes a well-aimed swipe at what he calls metaphorics.

> "Let us consider the "desktop metaphor," that opening screen jumble that is widely thought at the present time to be useful [...]"

> "Why is this curious clutter called a desktop? It doesn't *look* like a desktop; we have to tell the beginner *how* it looks like a desktop, because it doesn't (it might as easily properly be called the Tablecloth or the Graffiti Wall). [...]"

> "We are told to believe that this is a "metaphor" for a "desktop." But I have never personally seen a desktop where pointing at a lower piece of paper makes it jump to the top, or where placing a sheet of paper on top of a file folder causes the folder to gobble it up. I do not believe such desks exist; and I do not think I would want one if it did."

> Nelson (1990) p237.

So the analogous connection between a design and the outside world is often tenuous. But learning via analogical reasoning, bringing old knowledge structures to bear on new situations, can be seen as a basic human characteristic (Rumelhart and Norman, 1983), one on which we can capitalize (when it really exists). And imposing the same "metaphor" across operations does create consistency of operation, thus increasing transfer of learning, and fewer errors will be made with this kind of intuitive behaviour, though not necessarily because of the analogical force of any metaphorical design elements.

There is evidence that providing users with a clear metaphorical model, versus giving procedural instructions to carry out a task, leads to improved efficiency and memorability (Borgman, 1986a; Payne, 1987). But a metaphor will not match the operation of a system in all respects; adopting an inappropriate one is potentially very counter-productive (Halasz and Moran, 1982).

We can distinguish four different levels of analogy in interface design (cf. Hutchins, 1989):

- **The conceptual model** is the overall view of the system, or part of the system, as conceptualized by the designer or design team. This may comprise one overall metaphorical view, or may contain one or more metaphors, and non-metaphorical aspects, within it.

- **Mental models** are how users actually view the system, which will vary with the sophistication and experience of the user. This should hopefully be reasonably compatible with the Conceptual Model, but will not be identical in detail, nor will it be complete.

- **A metaphor** in this context is a mapping relation between aspects of the conceptual model and the world at large (e.g. a desktop).

- **Interaction modes** are details of user operation that are included in the conceptual model and may correlate with metaphors (clicking to open a file, dragging to move from one folder to another, uttering a word to place a marker, for example).

Level of mapping	Interaction events	Example metaphor	System perspective
5 Pragmatic	Tasks	Finding out about a topic	User session(s)
4 Semantic	Ways of doing tasks	Going on a library tour	Organized set of traversals
3 Syntactic	Combinations of moves/items	Selecting a book and 'opening' it	Displayed node
2 Lexical	Items/moves (icons, clicks, pointing, etc.)	Pointing at a picture	Input/output token recognized

Table 5.1 - Levels of system-metaphor mapping

5.2.1 Levels of Metaphor Mapping

We illustrate the different levels at which system functionalities and metaphor characteristics may map onto each other in Table 5.1 (inspired by Hammond and Allinson, 1987). Some of the characteristics at each level may provide a match (or a mismatch). A metaphor need not be appropriate at all levels of description. Indeed, a metaphor that is self-evidently inappropriate at some levels of description will be more successful than one that is ambiguous; mappings will not be attempted at inappropriate levels in the former case. However, the primary features of the metaphor should be present. System entities outside the metaphor will not detract unless the demarcation between what is in and out is not made clear.

Different metaphors at the same level of description within a design may be equally possible and the use of multiple metaphors may often be desirable (Weyer and Borning, 1985). The value of alternative approaches to a particular application needs to be tested empirically. Multiple metaphors are likely to be chosen for designs that attempt to present different, tailored, views on the knowledge base, to make these views intelligible to the same or different users. So within an educational hypertext context different formats, such as coffee-table book, adventure story, reference book, or documentary account might be chosen as alternative book-type metaphors at the pragmatic level of mapping (Koh and Chua, 1989). Different formats would imply the presentation of different portions of the knowledge base, such as a picture and caption sequence versus the presentation of detailed supporting material via access to comprehensive indices.

Once the idea of one overall metaphor is abandoned, alternative realizations of design concepts at several levels of mapping become more likely. Interaction with an adventure game based around playing the role of a helicopter pilot in a given geographical region (by directly piloting a simulated vehicle over the chosen terrain) is going to be significantly different, at many levels of mapping, from accessing a database of views of exactly the same region via a simulated photograph album. As we pointed out in the previous section, the choice of design should depend on the nature of the material and the task users will wish to achieve. Beyond these factors, artistic flair and imagination will contribute to the 'black art' of interface design, as always.

5.2.2   Problems with Metaphors

A single, over-detailed metaphor can be too restrictive and cumbersome. As suggested above, over-enforcement of metaphors may have the same effect (problems such as "I can't copy the contents of a set of folders unless I open each one", or "I can permanently lose the clock if I put it in the waste bin", for example). Some designers have deliberately enforced metaphors to restrict the flexibility with which users may interact with a system (e.g. Benest *et al.*, 1987). The justification is that in this case (a library-like representation) users are so familiar with an established way of accessing information that the electronic replacement must closely, some might say slavishly, mirror the original. But the price can be high in terms of flexibility and new possibilities.

Hammond and Allinson (1987) distinguish mapping abstraction, of primary metaphor entities, from mapping invocation, of secondary metaphor entities. The former are activated initially in an all-or-none fashion. The latter are generated later, in response to a perceived lack of knowledge. They involve mental work on the part of the user, and are under conscious control. The implication of this is that it is particularly important that primary entities suggested by the main metaphor should indeed be present, otherwise users are likely to make errors over which they have little control. We might expect it to be relatively safe to omit secondary metaphor entities.

Systems will have functionality beyond that embodied in real world metaphors and this should not be thrown away unnecessarily. Smith (1987) discusses the trade-off between features that correspond to the metaphorical model the interface is built around, so-called 'literal' features, and 'magic' aspects that deviate from that model and so reduce learnability, but provide extra, sometimes vital, power. Hammond and Allinson (1987) specifically examined the use of metaphorical versus magic features in their hypermedia tuition system built around a travel metaphor. Surprisingly, magic features did not present problems of recognition or use. Users did, however, falsely recognize features which corresponded to the metaphor but were actually not included in the system. Smith (1987) points to the importance of 'external' factors, unavoidable features which are neither magical nor metaphorical, as the most difficult for users to cope with. A good conceptual model is likely to contain metaphorical elements, and highly desirable magic features. But it is also likely, of necessity, to include less easily assimilated external factors.

An important determinant of what will work at the conceptual model level is the availability of input and output devices for modal level mapping. If, for example, 3-D modelling and presentation can be combined with appropriately sophisticated input devices for manipulation and exploration, a much broader range of possibilities for the use of metaphor presents itself than if the user is limited to pointing and typing at a conventional WIMP (window-icon-mouse-pointer) interface.

Clearly, metaphors must be chosen with great care, depending on the nature of the application and the availability of interaction devices. Non-metaphorical elements which are magical need not necessarily be problematic to users, but incorporating features within an overall model can have strong benefits. Badly chosen metaphors are very counter-productive, however. Users are likely to be confused when items suggested by metaphors are present but are not part of the conceptual design. An example of this would be where book choices are shown arranged on shelves, but the user must access them via a catalogue, rather than directly (the other side of the over-enforcement problem mentioned above). Metaphors may also be harmful when they simply do not match the users' mental model, by suggesting features which do not exist or blocking the use of existing features. For example, Halasz and Moran (1982) found that the analogy of a typewriter interfered with learning to use a word processor because of such a mismatch of features.

5.2.3   The Use of Metaphor in Hypermedia

Many existing hypermedia systems foster a mental model based around some sort of metaphor, such as an encyclopaedia, boxes of cards, or an electronic library. Many use a different, incompatible metaphor for presenting structure of information; typically graphs of some kind are used as an aid to navigation. The range of modes is quite impoverished, consisting of just a few navigational features, sometimes deliberately so (e.g Yoder *et al.*, 1989). This can be beneficial, if appropriate. But metaphors can be problematic. The cards-in-boxes model, for example, while adequate for many purposes and very easily mapped onto the underlying node and link structure of NoteCards, is not sufficient to allow material to be arranged in ways that reflect users real task needs (Halasz, 1988). Developing enhanced structural capability is obviously necessary to achieve the required ability to develop clusters of cards, but to make this usable would also need a richer conceptual model for the interface.

Future hypermedia systems will need a sophisticated, open-ended conceptual model, rich enough to fully support their enhanced functionality. Strong, explanatory metaphorical elements are likely to contribute significantly to this model. Hypermedia design provides one of the clearest examples of the need for metaphor, just because of the difficulty users are likely to encounter in forming coherent mental models of the system to support navigation and other forms of information retrieval. Even computer-mediated query is not unproblematic, and we have argued elsewhere that various styles of information retrieval will need to be smoothly, and coherently, integrated in future hypermedia systems (Waterworth and Chignell, 1989b). Metaphor provides a powerful approach to that integrative design process.

Designs should not be bounded by metaphors, however: they should improve on them, and here the need for experimentation, to determine just what is an improvement, is particularly strong. It is already clear that the conceptual model will need to contain non-metaphorical aspects where functional (e.g. magic features). So a hypermedia system built around the metaphor of a map, which can be explored to navigate a knowledge base of information about a certain geographical region, for example, might be enhanced with such magical features as 'time cars' - for comparing features at different periods of history - or a 'space warp' facility to juxtapose physically distant regions for purposes of comparison.

An important design question is whether or not it is preferable for a hypermedia system to adopt one dominant metaphor supporting the conceptual model, with features such as navigation techniques corresponding to this metaphor. Any deviations would need to be well-chosen. In our example above, cartographic layout may be seen as dominant, and the principal means of navigation (map tracing) might be expected to correspond to this model. On the other hand, there may be advantages to presenting the overall system as something new and different, thus a non-metaphorical conceptual model would represent the system as a whole, but incorporate various navigational features, both metaphorical and magic, as appropriate.

Metaphors in hypermedia (and in interface design in general) are generally partial. That is, parts of the real-world correspondence are included, parts are not. Such partial mappings of knowledge can be supported with no ambiguity, provided they are well chosen and the system is designed appropriately around them. And metaphors are only one way of improving interfaces. Metaphors can be combined, and often are. Different users will want more or less protection from the full complexity, and capability, of an interface. Some will be happy to work within the confines of a simple metaphor, others will want the full range of features available.

A single metaphor, or even a combination of metaphors, cannot cope with everything. At present, metaphors seem to be generated on a case by case basis. However, as we understand the basic dimensions of tasks better, it should be possible to develop libraries of complementary metaphors that operate at different levels of abstraction. Figure 5.1 represents an initial conceptualization of what a hierarchical library of metaphors might look like. At the top level, there will be a common inclusive metaphor such as a file system or a desktop. At a lower level, there will be a set of metaphor templates such as cards or books, which can then be specialized into task-specific metaphors as shown in the lowest level of the figure.

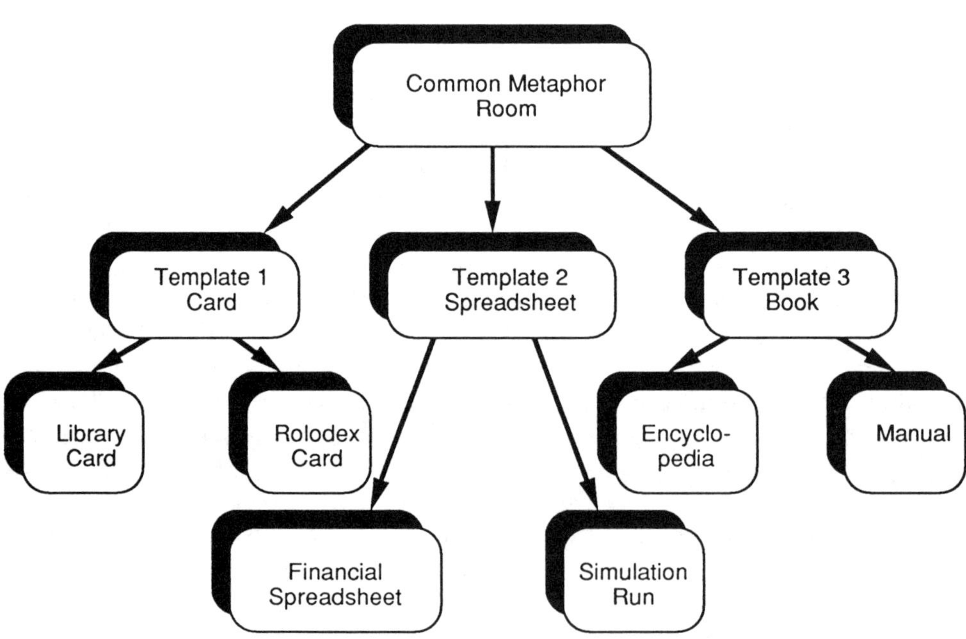

Figure 5.1 - A library of metaphors

The interface issues involved in using analogy to cater, in a flexible way, for users requiring different degrees of detail (information 'filters'), styles of presentation ('views' of the hyperbase) and complexity of interaction capability ('masks' on the interface) present serious challenges to designers. Indeed, it may not always be practical to attempt to fix all such design decisions in advance. Rather, the potential for adaptive change through the provision of dynamic hypermedia structuring is likely to be increasingly important in future, more advanced hypermedia systems.

5.3 DYNAMISM IN HYPERMEDIA

The distinction between static and dynamic hypermedia is fundamental. In static hypermedia, links are fixed during the authoring process. In dynamic hypermedia, links may be created at runtime using one of a number of processes. The ability to create links dynamically provides a virtual structuring feature for hypermedia that supplements the statically defined structure. The structural difference between static and dynamic hypermedia is illustrated in Figure 5.2 (after Parsaye *et al.*, 1989, figure 5.19). In static hypermedia, links between nodes are explicitly authored, whereas in dynamic hypermedia links may be created in a context-sensitive fashion in addition to being explicitly authored.

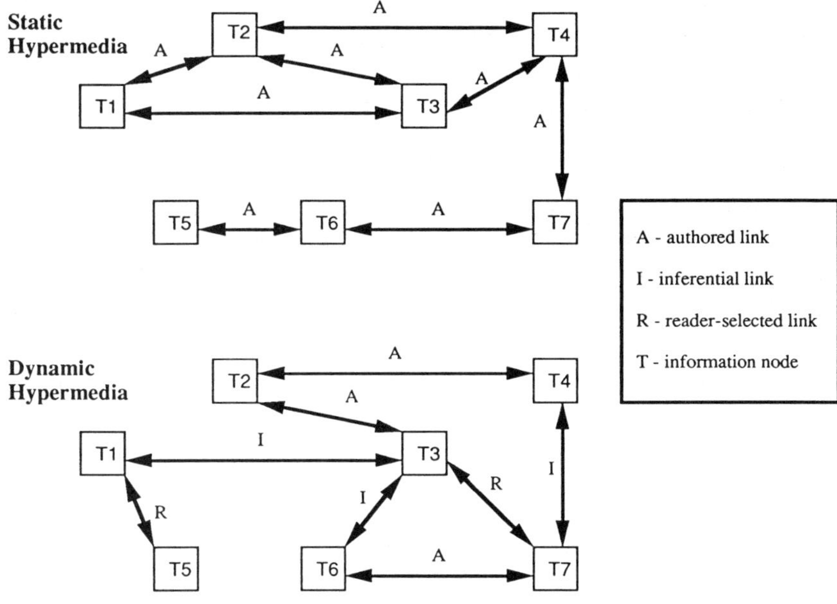

Figure 5.2 - Static and dynamic hypermedia

The concept of dynamic hypermedia embodies two main principles, a generative (or facilitative) principle that creates links, and an inhibitory (or filtering) principle that removes links. In the same way that one can build a sculpture by removing stone or by adding clay, one may construct dynamic hypermedia by removing existing links or by adding new links.

The main impact of dynamic hypermedia is that the structure of information is not fixed, and may consequently be adapted to changing contexts. Obviously, if the same set of links were always relevant, static structuring of hypermedia would be sufficient. A first step away from static hypermedia occurs in some systems when links are defined conditionally as only applying to certain types of user or certain types of situation. Webs or filters are then used to determine the conditions under which a link is applicable.

Since dynamic hypermedia is a new phenomenon, it is not clear how dynamism should be used to enhance the usability of hypermedia systems. The usage of a hypermedia system in general, and dynamism in particular, is closely related to the overall model of the system that one is trying to create. Dynamism has to be motivated by task-oriented goals, and the dynamic generation or filtering of links should be demonstrably superior to an equivalent static representation where fixed (pre-compiled) links are used to carry out the task.

5.3.1 An Example Application

The concept of dynamic hypermedia can perhaps best be understood with reference to an actual application. We have been experimenting with the ideas above in the development of a hypermedia-based information system that deals with the Japanese occupation of Singapore during World War II (Koh and Chua, 1989). In this system, reasons for selecting links (dynamically) include: (i) nodes sharing index terms (e.g. two nodes refer to General Yamashita), (ii) nodes sharing perspectives (e.g. they would both be of concern to a Japanese soldier or to a local Chinese), and (iii) both nodes being relevant when answering a question.

One example of this last method for selecting a link is as follows. A node that described an eye witness account of death and destruction, and a node that described the behaviour of army deserters might both be relevant to a question about the condition of Singapore City at the time of the British Surrender. As a second example, the topics Singapore and Pearl Harbour might be linked by a question such as:

"Which locations were vital to Japan's strategy of obtaining vital resources
such as oil and rubber through force?"

The use of questioning helps to give a goal orientation to hypermedia usage. One of
the problems with static hypermedia is that it seems to be consistent with a grazing
view of information browsing where information is looked at for no particular reason,
or because of general interest rather than in response to task goals. Questions can
be used to embody instructional or information seeking goals. Seen in this way,
hypermedia also becomes a way of carrying out computer-mediated information
retrieval, with a descriptive style of interaction, that requires the system to know
when to ask questions and what questions to ask. For instance, in a learning support
environment, some of the motivations for asking a question include:

(a) The prerequisite of knowing that the student either has enough
knowledge to answer the question directly or is capable of finding the
appropriate information.

(b) Stimulating "a line of thinking"; thus a question of this type may be
asked if the student appears to be wandering through the system
aimlessly, etc.

(c) Evaluation; the system should monitor its own performance and the
performance of the student. The system may then be dynamically configured
for students having different profiles based on user behaviour and
corresponding user models.

One approach to dynamic hypermedia and information seeking is to emphasize the
role of inference. However, in many cases, it seems that the role of creating dynamic
links can actually be handled by clever indexing. For instance, if we explicitly
represent the question about Japan's strategic interests and then represent topics
that are relevant to the answer (such as Singapore and Pearl Harbour) as keywords,
we can then create a link based on shared keywords (a similar strategy is used by
Salomon *et al.*, 1989, in defining links for guides). What this demonstrates is that it is
not the process of inferencing per se that is critical to the creation of dynamic links,
but rather it is the knowledge that will be used, whether it be via indexing or by
inferencing.

5.4 DESIGNING INTERFACES: PROBLEMS AND EXAMPLES

5.4.1 Why is Design Difficult?

Designers generally find the problem of creating satisfactory interfaces for hypermedia applications difficult. There seem to be three main reasons for this. Firstly, hypermedia structures are amorphous, integrating diverse heterogenous material which often lacks a clear underlying theme. Secondly, users of these systems typically have the responsibility for navigating around the available information. In a sense, they are placed inside the information structure itself, since the interface penetrates deeper into the content of the system than is the case with more conventional computer applications. Finally, there are no obvious parallels in the outside world on which a clearly metaphorical model can be based. So design approaches often seem arbitrary or do not map very well onto users' knowledge of the everyday world (i.e. the conceptual model does not readily conjure up an appropriate mental model in the minds of users). Where designs have been successful, it has generally been the case that the hypermedia system in question has relatively limited scope and functionality. There is often a trade-off between functionality and intelligibility.

Existing hypermedia systems display a remarkable variety of design approaches. In fact, the effort to create hypermedia systems can be characterized as a distributed and uncontrolled experiment in applied epistemology/ontology. Groups of researchers and developers have been busy creating various network representations of knowledge and calling it hypertext or hypermedia. Once the idea of hypertext became fashionable everyone felt quite happy to represent things in almost any way they wanted to, and the neat semantic nets of AI in the late 1970s have become a kind of hypermedia mayhem of the 1990s.

It is far from clear where all this is leading to. Perhaps someone will analyze the results of the experiment after a suitable length of time and make interesting observations about the consensus model of hypertext that is in use, the variety of link types that can be reasonably be used, and the relationship between hypertext, knowledge representation, and our world view in general. This seems unlikely; the experiment is too uncontrolled, and there is no reason to anticipate the emergence of a consensus.

For one thing, the application area is clearly crucial in determining what comprises an appropriate model. The field of structured design has led naturally enough to argumentation stuctures, as found first in the gIBIS system (Conklin, 1987) and later in hypermedia systems designed for the purpose of argumentation itself (e.g. Streitz *et al.*, 1989). Project management and collaborative work concerns have led to approaches based on the notion of "Speech Acts" (Searle, 1969), such as The Coordinator (Winograd and Flores, 1986). Documentation tasks tend to lead to book-like structures such as SuperBook (Egan et al, 1989). Educational aims have taken hypermedia in the direction of conditional links and user modelling.

There is certainly plenty of "data" out there, with all the hypertext models and systems that have been proposed or used in the last five years. Unfortunately, too little organized data collection has gone on, partly because few existing systems have yet been applied in earnest to realistic applications. Indeed, it sometimes seems that there are as many, or even more, systems in existence than there are users who have actually worked with them.

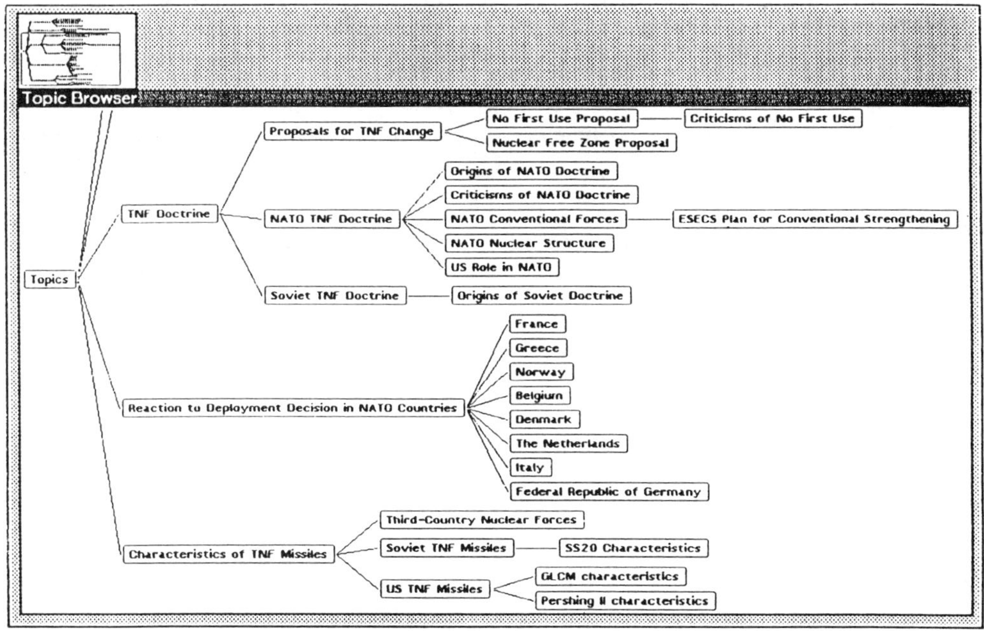

Figure 5.3 - Browser of a NoteCards FileBox hierarchy
(from Halasz, 1987)

5.4.2   Example Interfaces

Despite the sceptical tone of the last paragraph, it is instructive to examine a few of the interface designs that have emerged for hypermedia systems in recent years in detail. The figures below illustrate seven different hypermedia interfaces. Figure 5.3 shows the NoteCards browser which has a strong feel of computer science about it, and depends on the information in the system being arranged in a hierarchy that can readily be represented with this tree-like structure.

In contrast, Figure 5.4 illustrates the York University "hitchhiker" metaphor (Hammond and Allinson, 1988) applied to material on the topic of divided attention. In the upper screen, the user is confronted with a choice of either selecting a tour bus for passive exploration of the topic, or of selecting to see a summary of the topic or a list of relevant demonstrations. A range of other tools and options are provided as boxes along the bottom of the screen. Having selected the map button, the user is shown the lower screen and can then select a particular node of information to view.

Perhaps the most obvious way to implement a metaphorical model is to portray quite closely an existing physical reality. The interface shown in Figure 5.5 was clearly designed by a Macintosh enthusiast. In this world, everything is an object in a Mac-based office environment. In other words, the world of the interface maps very directly onto the world of a workroom. All objects in the world are buttons. Thus, we might click on the globe to view maps of the world, select the calculator or telephone from the desktop when we want to use those tools, access files from the filing cabinet against the wall, check the mail by clicking on the stack of letters in the lower left corner, look up a word in the dictionary or a number in the telephone directory, and so on.

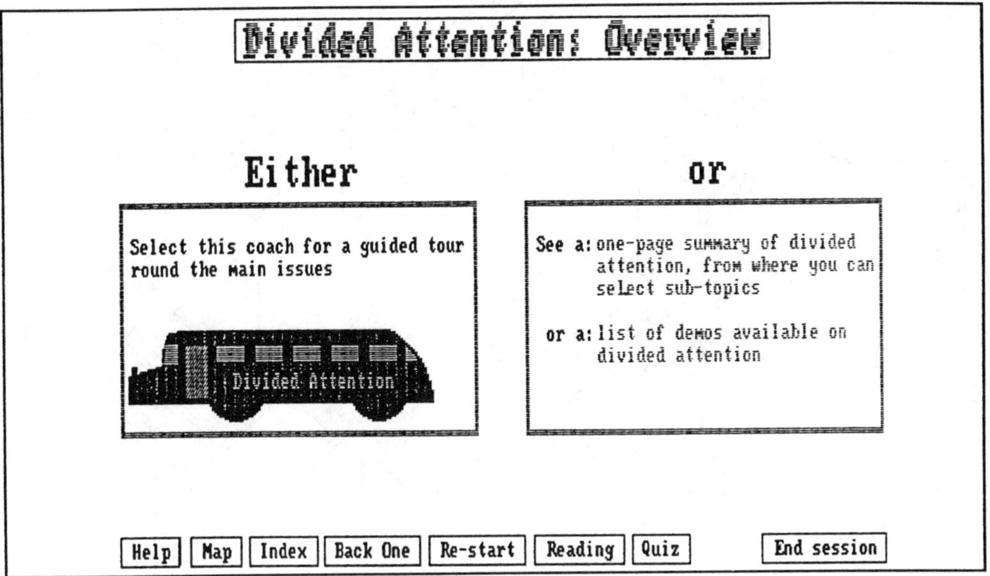

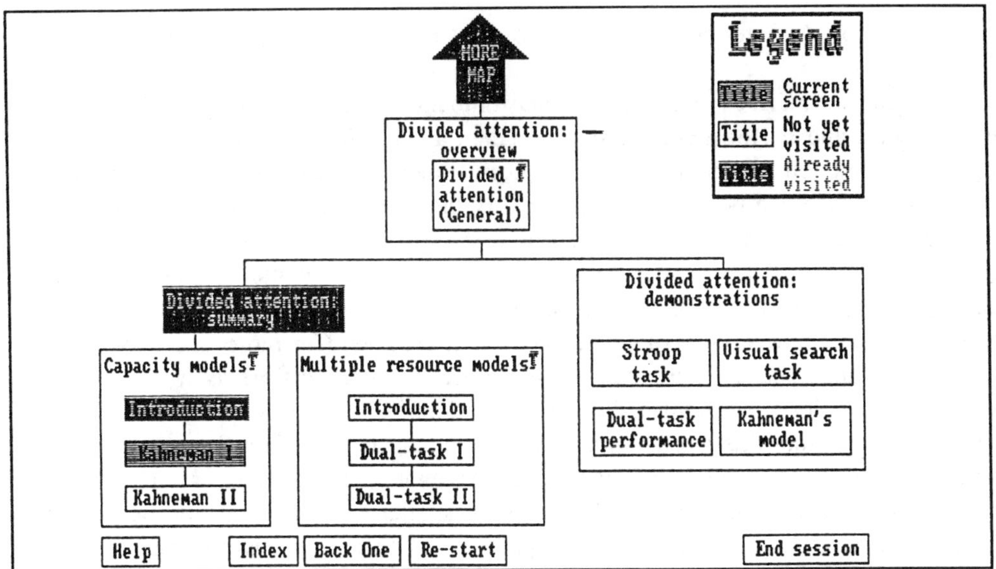

Figure 5.4 - Example screens from the York hypermedia system
(from Hammond and Allinson, 1988)

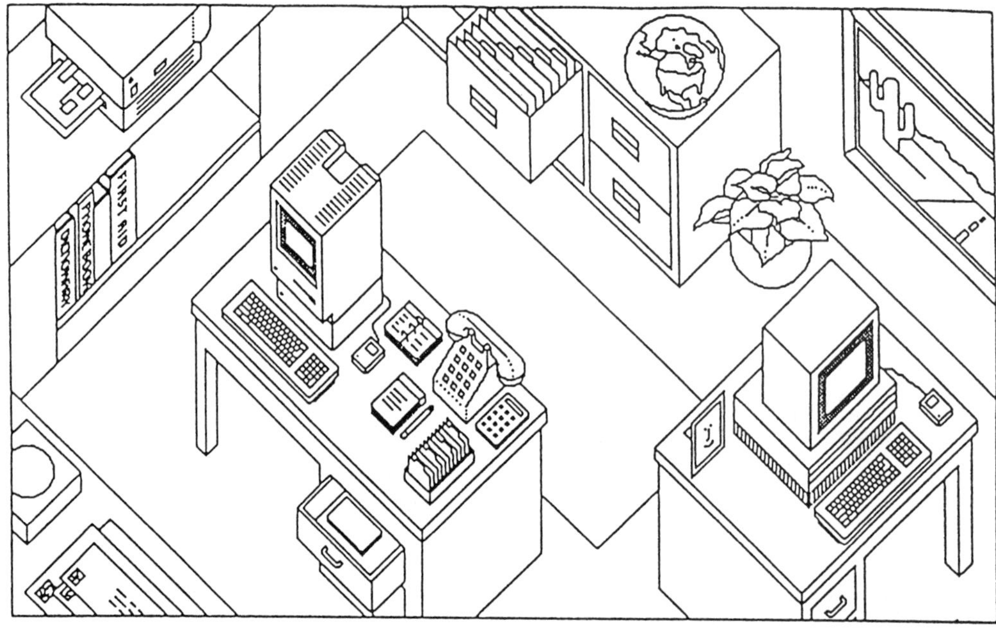

Figure 5.5 - An interface of graphical objects representing a real-world office

This idea of the interface as a life-like environment in which the user can locate and select objects and perform actions can be taken a stage further, by using techniques such as 3-D modelling and video to add extra dimensions and even greater realism. Then the interface can become a virtual reality that can be explored in the same way that we can move around real space. Figure 5.6 attempts to convey what such an interface might look at from the distance. In fact, the user would be presented with constantly changing views of this virtual world as he travels through the air above the city (gaining an overview of contents) or at street level (for more detail) or within buildings or open spaces. The user might choose to travel in time as well as space, since virtual reality is not confined to the limitations we experience in the real world. We can imagine that this hypothetical interface would be excellent for, say, a tourist guide to a city, or for students of architecture or town planning. But it seems unlikely that an approach so closely tied to the notion of spatial exploration would be suitable for a broad range of applications. To expand its usefulness we would have to start adding magic features appropriate to our target application. We discuss the issue of virtual worlds again in Chapter 8.

Figure 5.6 - Interface as 3-D virtual world

For narrowly circumscribed applications, a more focused approach to interface features will result in more specialized designs. Figure 5.7 shows two views of the interface of Glasgow Online (Baird and Percival, 1989). The top-level screen illustrates what might be called a chocolate box metaphor. All the available items are laid out for selection, with none given priority. Users simply select what they want from the tray of items. This works well when there are a relatively small number of options available. Having made this initial selection, the lower level screens maintain the metaphor to some extent. Basically, the interface always comprises a menu from which the user may select one item. As we have seen, menus work well for novice users when there are relatively few items at each menu level, and preferably not too many levels.

In Figure 5.8 we illustrate a somewhat more sophisticated interface, based around the metaphor of floor plans within a building. The system was designed for an Open House event at ISS. Our aim was to convey several, interrelated pieces of information: the physical layout of the three-storey building, information on projects, information on staff, organizational information, events of the day, and so on. For each of these categories we had textual material and images, for some we had sound recordings and graphics. We sought to design a system where the strong metaphor of the physical structure of the building would allow users to predict where and how to access all of these different pieces of information. In practice, however, we found it necessary to augment the model with several magic features, such as the browser control panel and the special-purpose buttons on the bottom right of the upper screen. We used an image of a jukebox (top right) as a button to access the lower screen, we allowed users to play a particular selection of music, adjust the volume, and turn background music on or off. The Macintosh screen at the left ran the production credits while a musical selection was playing.

How much did our main metaphor add or detract from the usability of the system? To answer this question definitively would require a more carefully controlled experiment than we were able to carry out. Certainly the system was very popular and most users seemed able to find their way around the range of available contents. We adapted the software we had created to meet the needs of a different application, that of an interactive system about the Life and Music of Zubir Said, the composer of Singapore's national anthem "Majulah Singapura" (see Loo and Chung, 1991). Many of the elements contained in the interface of the earlier system were retained, such as the topic and browse buttons along the bottom of the screen (although these were redesigned; see Figure 5.9). We also retained the idea of a jukebox icon that gave access to a user-controlled "jukebox" on which a selection of the composer's music could be played.

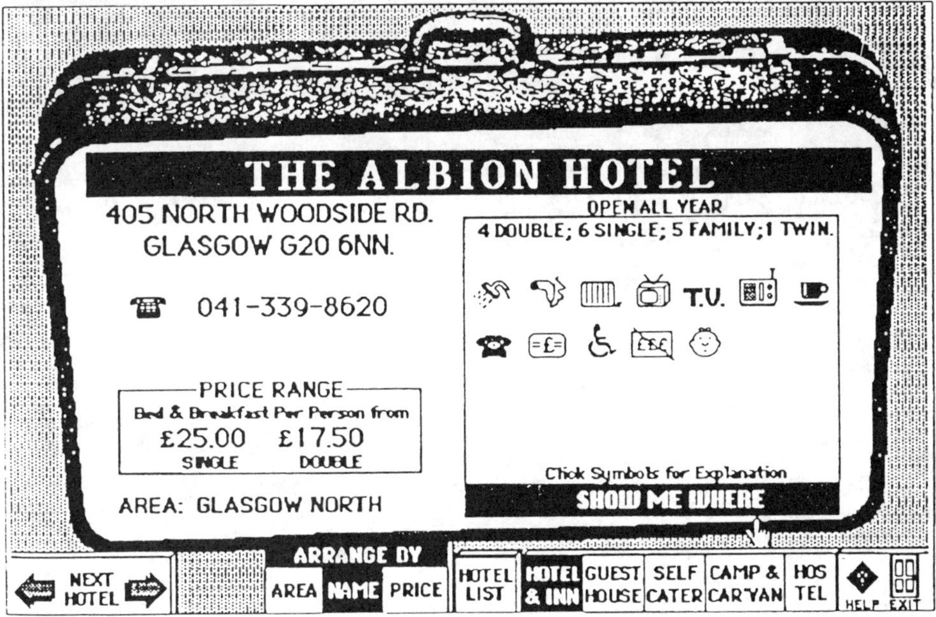

Figure 5.7 - Two levels of the Glasgow Online user interface

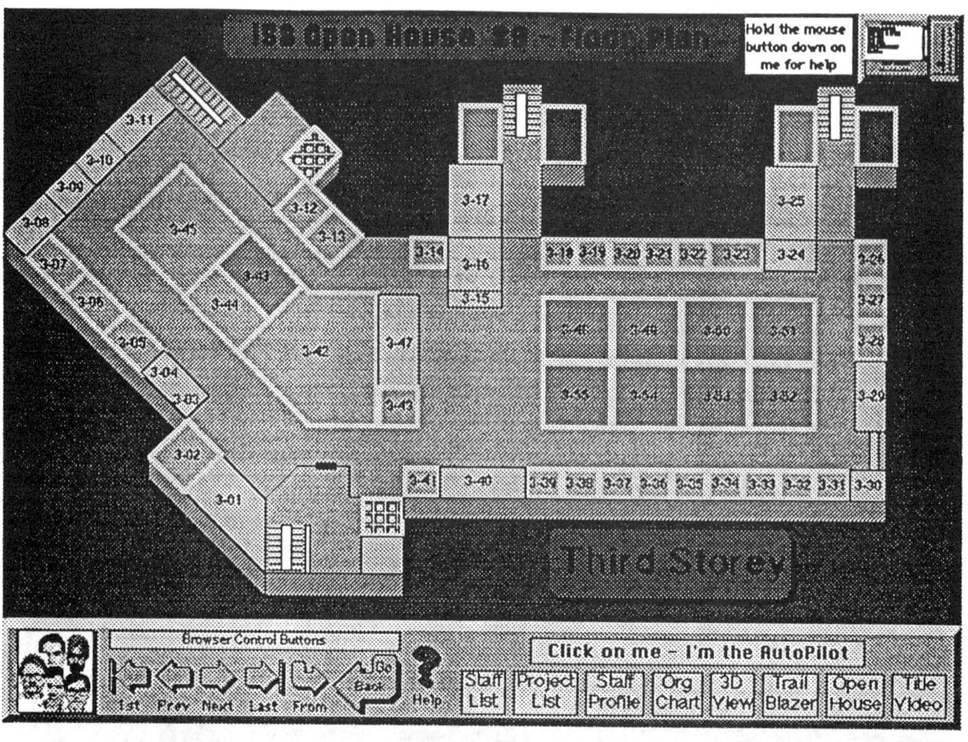

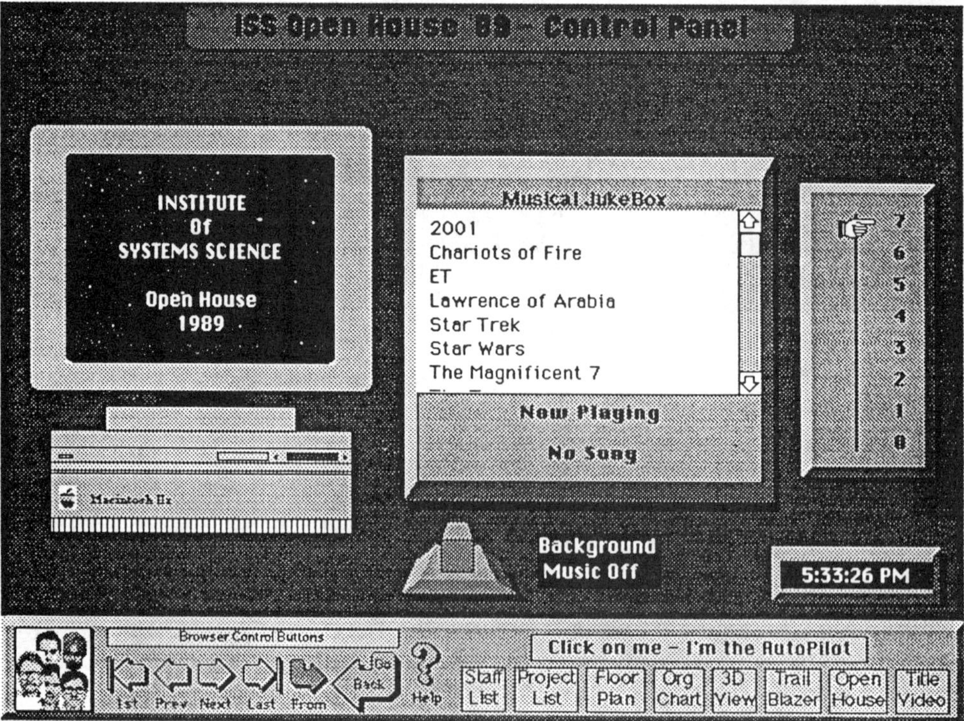

Figure 5.8 - Two views of the ISS Open House system

The Zubir Said system was part of a public exhibition about the composer organized by the National Museum of Singapore. It was very successful in this role and was very heavily used by a broad range of visitors to the exhibition. What is noteworthy was that, apart from the jukebox concept, the Zubir Said system abandoned the overall interface metaphor of floor plans (since this was inappropriate) and did not substitute another. Rather than developing such a model, attention was focused on making the interface clear, consistent, and with components that were themselves easy to understand. This worked well, although some features of the system, such as hypermedia links between pages and to pop-up annotations were little used. We ascribed this to the fact that these individual features were not obvious, nor was there any encouragement to experiment from a suggestive model. In the earlier system with floor plans, users were naturally tempted to click on locations shown on the plan, which results in their following a link to a related node of information, such as information on the staff member accommodated in that room, or details of a project carried out in a particular laboratory.

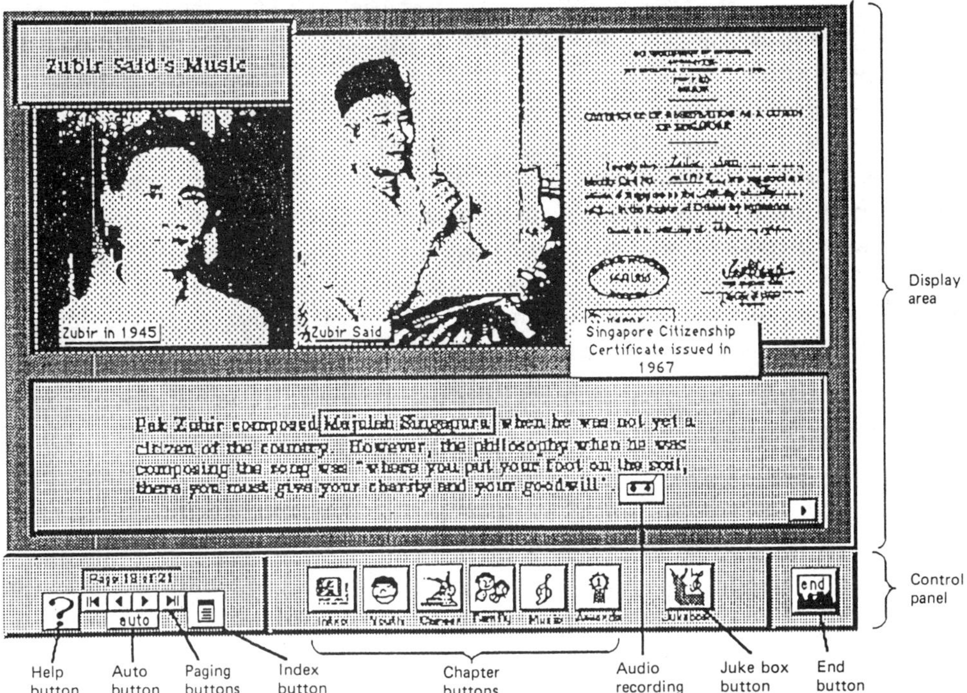

Figure 5.9 - Interface of the Zubir Said system

It seems that metaphor can enhance the usability of a system if there is a natural match between that metaphor and the application focus. But an interface can seldom, if ever, be based entirely around a single metaphor. And sometimes a non-metaphorical interface, with well-designed features, will work better than one based on a metaphor but which does not match the application well enough to allow users to make predictions or suggest to them experiments they might try.

5.5   CONCLUSIONS

It is clear that there are many unanswered questions about how hypermedia systems may be constructed to be more usable and effective. At present there are relatively few research findings that can assist in answering these questions. In spite of these concerns, it is possible to discern key directions for hypermedia usability research. These directions, summarized below, derive from the properties of hypermedia interfaces as extensions of conventional interfaces, and the interaction of those properties with advanced technologies for representing knowledge and structure within the interface.

Research issues derived from conventional interfaces include metaphors and structuredness. In general there will be a necessary interaction between these two dimensions, since at some level a metaphor should capture or account for the structure of the application or information that it describes.

Metaphors provide a way of making the structure of hypermedia intuitively recognisable. We need to find the best metaphors to maximize the effectiveness of navigation and computer-mediated information retrieval. At present, there is a tendency to separate different information seeking functions into separate and distinct types of information retrieval environment. The design of metaphors that enhance usability is one of the most important issues facing both hypermedia design and interface design in general.

Structuredness within hypermedia reflects the degree to which different types of nodes and links are available. By utilizing a variety of types it is possible to define a continuum of structuredness that ranges from "pure" hypermedia that consists only of homogeneous nodes and associative links to highly structured environments such as relational databases and hierarchically organized information systems. The effects of structuredness on usability will be influenced by the type of task being carried out, the type of visualization and navigation tools available, and the type of user.

The notions of relevance and importance address the issue of assisting information seeking within hypermedia applications. Relevance is a vital factor in cognition and communication, and is conspicuous by its absence in current hypermedia systems. Relevance-importance is a dimension that may be utilized in the development of navigation tools. The relevance of nodes and links in context, and the importance (global relevance) of nodes and links considered across the network, lead to an actively changing representation of structure. Clearly, representation should reflect this dimension.

Graphical and spatial representation will not work well if relevance and importance are not reflected. Space is not intrinsically memorable; we do not remember a landscape of labelled, identical apartment blocks, for example. The work of Eleanor Rosch, in particular (e.g., Rosch and Mervis, 1975; Rosch *et al.*, 1976) has shown how important concepts such as importance (salience) and typicality are in human organization of conceptual structures. We remember our way around in terms of important features. It seems likely that important items in hypermedia should be large and distinctively shaped, as are well-known landmark buildings in the physical environment of a city. Similarly, related items should probably share distinctive features or be related by proximity.

The existence of nodes that vary in relevance and importance provides a basis for the development of navigation tools that enhance the usability of hypermedia. Visualization is a related dimension that also contributes to the development of navigation tools.

Visualization is concerned with the way in which information, or information structure, is conveyed to the user in visual form. Visualization ranges from simple graphical representations of node and link structure to complex 3-D representations of hypermedia networks. There is obviously considerable interaction between the visualization methods and metaphors that are used in hypermedia applications.

The last two directions for research we considered were concerned with dynamism in hypermedia. Dynamism itself is an important dimension of usability, as is the interaction model knowledge that makes the implementation of dynamism possible.

Hypermedia may be static, where nodes, links, and interaction models are fixed and pre-compiled in some authoring process, or dynamic. Various degrees of dynamism are possible depending on whether or not nodes, links, or interaction models may be defined at runtime. In addition, different types of dynamism may be used to make this runtime configuration possible. Development of self-configuring representations for browsing (and query) within hypermedia may be based on richness of connections and on past retrieval patterns, thus integrating structure and search in the interface representation. Screens or filters may also be used to configure hypermedia for particular users and types of tasks.

The interaction model of an interface consists of the evaluative loop that regulates the dialogue or series of transactions between user and hypermedia system. Interaction models range from simple point and click models, that occur in undifferentiated browsing, to complex knowledge-based models such as might occur in a CAL environment that implements tutorial strategies based on sophisticated pedagogic knowledge.

The demands of information seeking in an information-rich environment require us to think about structure, browsing and information retrieval in new ways. The passive nature of current hypermedia systems will have to give way to a more actively helpful approach. At present, hypermedia allows us to create vast networks of association, but does not help us interpret this network (Jones, 1987). It is something of a paradox that the ability to browse is regarded as one of the major reasons for using hypermedia and yet there are no satisfactory models of what browsing consists of and how it should be carried out. The best way of representing information in a browser is simply not known. Aspects of locating and browsing items in multimedia information systems are discussed in detail in the next chapter.

Chapter 6

Exploring Multimedia Information

with Mark H Chignell

"Next time you see a lie being spread or a bad decision being made out of sheer ignorance, pause, and think of hypertext."

K. Eric Drexler, *Engines of Creation*

6.1   INTRODUCTION

Despite the currency of broad definitions of information retrieval such as that of Salton and McGill (1983): "Information retrieval is concerned with the representation, storage, organization, and accessing of information items", the concept has become closely related with keyword-based querying of indexed bibliographic databases using Boolean logic. However, information exploration is a broader activity that is carried out in a variety of ways by different people (elsewhere we refer to this as 'information seeking'; see Waterworth and Chignell, 1989a). For instance, browsing, whether through books, library shelves, or hypermedia documents is a form of exploration activity. Our main goal in this chapter is to introduce a model (Waterworth and Chignell, 1991) that covers a broad range of information exploration styles and strategies, because information exploration is at the very heart of multimedia interaction.

What do we mean to convey by the term 'information exploration'? In a recently published dictionary based on current British usage (COBUILD, 1987), the word 'explore' is defined as follows: "If you explore a place, you travel there because you have not been there before, or because nobody has been there before, in order to find out what it is like". So a key element of exploration according to common usage of the term is the notion of travelling to a region to find what (information) is located there. If one is actively concerned with selecting the route to a given location during the process of exploration, then one can be said to be engaged in navigation: "If you navigate, you work out which direction to go while you are travelling..." (COBUILD, 1987). From hypermedia enthusiasts, we frequently hear the terms 'navigate' and 'browse' used synonymously. But this obscures an important distinction between choosing routes and the reasons for making those choices. Contrast the definition of 'browse' with that of 'navigate' above: "If you browse you look at several things ... in a casual, unhurried way, in the hope that you might find something interesting" (COBUILD, 1987). By our account, browsing is opposed to querying, which we would redefine as "exploration with a specific target in mind".

Our model of information exploration brings out this important distinction between responsibility for selecting routes and the purpose of the exploratory behaviour. We also resolve a long-standing confusion between these two aspects of locating information and the manner in which choices made during exploration are expressed, i.e. the interaction method. We go on to illustrate the use of the model with paradigmatic examples of each type of exploration behaviour, and with a preliminary experiment that examines the effectiveness of different types of information exploration.

After the model description and experimental test we then address the issue of how information exploration systems may be developed. We propose an extended model of hypermedia that includes mediated search, along with a referential style of querying based on index linking that may provide a smooth transition between browsing and querying. We conclude with a discussion of patterns of exploration behaviour, showing how Ellis's (1989) model of information seeking may be incorporated within our information exploration approach.

6.2   A THREE-DIMENSIONAL MODEL OF INFORMATION EXPLORATION

6.2.1   Structural Responsibility

Discussions concerning user interfaces to information technology tend to blur distinctions between user perspectives on the task and the perspective from the system's point of view. For instance, the apparently intuitive concept of navigation reflects this distinction. Navigation is unstructured from the system perspective but structured from the user perspective. This dichotomy is a direct result of which agent (i.e. the user or the system) is responsible for carrying out search. In the case of navigation, users are responsible for controlling the search process and as a result it is they, rather than the system, that must be aware of the structure of the information. This role is reversed in the case of traditional information retrieval, where it is the system that is responsible for searching and which must consequently be concerned with structure. The issue of who is concerned with structure represents a primary dimension of exploration that we will refer to as *structural responsibility*.

6.2.2   Target Orientation

We find evidence for a second dimension of exploration in contrasting the activities of browsing and querying. Browsing is distinguished from querying by the absence of a definite target in the mind of the user. We refer to this second dimension of exploration as *target orientation*. Thus the distinction between browsing and querying is not determined by the actions of the user, or by the configuration of the system, but by the cognitive state of the user. Presumably, there is a continuum of user behaviours varying between querying and browsing that is characterized by the level of specificity of the user's informational goals. Given the existence of this continuum, it may be inappropriate to arbitrarily classify user behaviour as either browsing or querying and build systems that reflect this strict dichotomy. This view of browsing suggests the need to merge conventional information retrieval with browsing, rather than the seemingly prevalent view that browsing is best implemented as user search within an unstructured (associative) network.

The view that browsing involves an absence of target specificity in search is orthogonal to the distinction between navigation and information retrieval. Thus our analysis has so far revealed two dimensions of information exploration in hypermedia systems. The definition of browsing focuses on the distinction between targeted and discovery-based information exploration. In contrast, the definition of navigation emphasizes the responsibility of the user, as opposed to the system, for dealing with structure.

Since, as we have defined them, these two dimensions are clearly orthogonal, both browsing and querying can occur as part of navigation or information retrieval processes. Thus users may use queries for navigation (although this possibility has generally been ignored in previous approaches to hypermedia and information retrieval), and may be said to browse the contents of a database using information retrieval techniques. This indicates four distinct exploratory activities that may occur (see Table 6.1) but, as we discuss below, it is possible to develop combinations of these activities that represent intermediate points on the respective dimensions.

	Targetted	Discovery
User handles structure	NAVIGATIONAL QUERY	NAVIGATIONAL BROWSE
System handles structure	MEDIATED QUERY	MEDIATED BROWSE

Table 6.1 - Two dimensions of information exploration

6.2.3   Interaction Method

A third dimension of exploration arises from the method of interaction used in the interface to the information system. While methods of interaction may be differentiated in various ways, a major distinction can be drawn between descriptive interfaces, where the user describes what is wanted, and referential forms of interaction, where the user selects or refers to what is wanted (generally using some variant of a menu). Descriptive interfaces have generally been associated with querying behaviour in traditional information retrieval style, whereas referential interfaces have generally been associated with browsing during navigation, but there is no intrinsic correlation between the interaction method and target orientation or structural responsibility. Thus we have a third dimension of information exploration, *interaction method,* as shown in Figure 6.1.

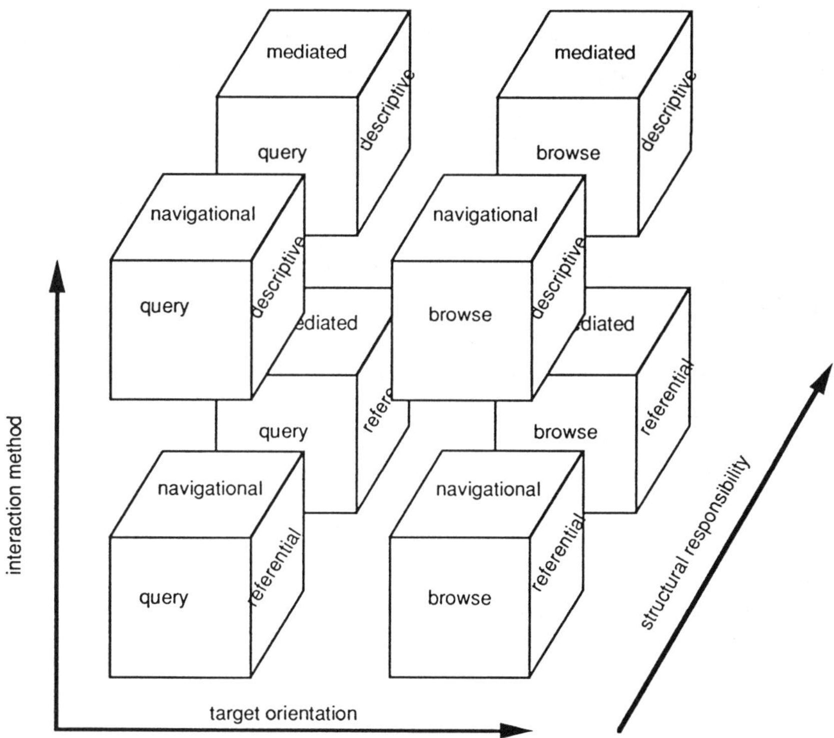

Figure 6.1 - Three dimensions of information exploration

In our view, this three dimensional model clarifies the role of concepts such as navigation, browsing and querying in terms of fundamental components of information exploration. Other approaches tend to incorporate both structural awareness (on the part of the user) and a discovery target orientation within the definition of navigation as an activity. By focusing on navigation as a process where structural responsibility rests with the user, and contrasting it with mediated search, it is possible to consider research approaches to improving the effectiveness of browsing and navigation such as:

(i) Increase navigation effectiveness by increasing the awareness of structure.

(ii) Increase the effectiveness of browsing by assisting the process of choosing between different elements in the current structure.

The fundamental problem of navigational browsing as defined here is that one has to decide on where to go next within an information structure without having a clear a priori target in mind. This places a great deal of reliance on the immediate context of the surrounding structure in navigation decisions. Navigation requires an awareness of what the structure is and a familiar, or easily usable, mechanism for selecting where to go next based on that awareness.

6.3 PARADIGMATIC EXAMPLES OF INFORMATION EXPLORATION

In this section we describe various examples of information exploration in terms of our model. For present purposes we ignore the role of interaction method which, as we noted earlier, is orthogonal to our other two dimensions. We thus focus here on four styles of exploration:

(i) navigational browsing,
(ii) navigational querying,
(iii) mediated browsing, and
(iv) mediated querying.

6.3.1   Navigational Browsing

Discussions of users interacting with hypertext systems typically assume a type of navigational browsing (e.g. Yankelovich *et al.*, 1988) where one topic tends to lead into another. In this type of exploration the user is moving through the information without a clear target in mind. Often in this type of situation there is a motivation to find information, but the user has the sense that while he cannot formulate his information need as a query, he will recognize relevant information when he sees it.

Consider the case of someone who wants to write an essay on Renaissance painting and the cultural influences that affected it. The following is an example of a navigational browsing style of interaction. Note that we are not necessarily concerned with any system actually in existence, but rather with how a form of navigational browsing might be implemented in principle.

The user is presented with a menu of topics, and chooses - *Artists*.

The user is presented with a choice of different categories of artist, and chooses - *Renaissance painters*.

Note here that we are already carrying out navigation, even though we are using menus. This is because the user is interacting directly with the system structure. The question of whether the user is browsing or not at this stage is a little more problematic. In some senses the user is operating in a querying fashion since the topic of "Renaissance art"is in fact a target, but within this topic the user will have to browse. Thus in this example the user navigates to the topic neighbourhood in a querying fashion and then browses for information within that neighbourhood. This two-stage type of information exploration (where one finds the neighbourhood first) appears to be a useful strategy for dealing with large amounts of information (Shute *et al.*, 1986). Browsing within a well-defined subtopic (neighbourhood) will generally be much more efficient than browsing the complete information system.

The system shows a menu of Renaissance painters, the user chooses - *Michelangelo*

At this point the Michelangelo "node" is displayed and the user finds out that Michelangelo was a sculptor as well as a painter.

The system shows links leading to a number of topics on Michelangelo, the user chooses - *Sistine Chapel*

The user now reads the information on this topic and finds out that one of Michelangelo's masterpieces (the ceiling of the Sistine Chapel) was commissioned by the church, thereby explaining the content of that work. By browsing information on other Renaissance painters he will find a similar influence. Depending on what information is available, he may also discover that the sponsors of paintings often appeared along with members of their families as historical or biblical figures in the paintings. Thus by browsing the information, the user might eventually reach the conclusion that Renaissance art was strongly affected by religious subjects and by the economics of sponsors and their preferences.

This example demonstrates that querying may precede browsing in information exploration, and that relevant information may be obtained even when a target is not clearly defined a priori.

6.3.2　Navigational Querying

In the next paradigmatic example of exploration, an a priori target is present, but the style of search is still navigational. Assume that we again have an information system on artists, where different pieces of information are connected by menus and reference links. In this example, the user knows that he wants to get information on the religious influence on Renaissance art. In this case, rather than choosing renaissance artists, he might begin by choosing "art and religion" to get an appropriate background on the topic. He might then choose a topic such as

"Christian art prior to 1600."

The point here is that navigation, whether it be through menu selection or link selection, is actually a process of choosing where to go next. In any exploration situation the user will actually be somewhere on the continuum between knowing exactly what they want to find (querying) and having only an extremely vague idea of what they are looking for (browsing). Thus in our navigational query example, the user has a more detailed definition of his own requirements. In the case of navigational browsing he only knew that he was looking for cultural influences on Renaissance art, whereas with navigational querying he could define the topic fairly precisely. In both cases though, the search mechanism involved direct choices by the user (where the choices could be amongst menu items or links).

6.3.3   Mediated Browsing

In the case of mediated browsing our hypothetical user again knows only that he wants to get information on cultural influences on Renaissance art. The difference here though is the agent of search, which has now become the system rather than, as in navigation, the user. So the user makes queries instead of navigational choices. Thus the effective question that the system poses the user at each point in the search is not "where do you want to go next?" but "what sort of information do you want me to get?". Thus we might have the following interaction:

User: Search Renaissance

System: Over 200 topics retrieved, be more specific

User: Search Renaissance and Art

System: The following topics were retrieved:

> *1. Perspective in Renaissance Art*
> *2. Leonardo da Vinci*
> *3. The golden age of Florence*

After reading about interesting-looking topics, the user might refine the query until the topic became clearer to him or until he has viewed a sufficient number of information items for his purpose.

6.3.4   Mediated Querying

In mediated querying the user has a much better sense of what the target of the search is. Presumably this will allow better specification of the query, provided that there is some understanding of how to form the query, what descriptors are appropriate, and so on. There is plenty of evidence, however, to suggest that querying approaches such as Boolean retrieval are difficult for many users (e.g. Borgman, 1986b) and thus navigation may be needed as a supplement to mediated search, even in cases where the user knows what the information target is.

In the following cases we show examples of successful and unsuccessful mediated querying.

User: search (Renaissance and Art) and (Religion or Christianity)

System: the following nodes are retrieved.

> *1. art in churches*
> *2. church sponsorship of Art*
> *3. Islamic art during the Renaissance*
> *4. the Sistine Chapel*

Notice that in this example the user formed a query that directly produced relevant information. In other examples there might be some trial and error in getting the right query. For instance,

User: search Renaissance

System: More than 200 topics retrieved, please be more specific

or

User: search Renaissance and Religion and Christianity

System: No topics retrieved.

These examples illustrate both the good and bad features of mediated querying. Firstly, if the information has been indexed the right way, a good query might get you straight to the relevant information. On the other hand, the demands of building the right query can hinder searching in some cases. For instance, in the example above, the user appears to be using the AND operator (Religion and Christianity) when really they should probably be using "or". This is a fairly common problem in naive searchers.

6.4 EXPERIMENTAL COMPARISON OF FOUR EXPLORATION STYLES

As an example of a study that attempted to clarify some of the issues we have raised, we briefly describe in this section an initial experiment on exploration styles in relation to task demands. In fact, this serves to illustrate the difficulties of empirical work in this area, though we remain convinced of the need for further behavioural work.

In this study we compared users' performance in solving two types of problem when forced to adopt either a mediated or a navigational style of exploration. The problems were designed to encourage either a browsing or a querying approach, since one set of problems were meant to require more interpretive answers than a second set. In other words, we were testing the following four combinations:

>   (i) Enforced mediated search with 'query' problems,
>   (ii) Enforced mediated search with 'browse' problems,
>   (iii) Enforced navigation with 'query' problems, and
>   (iv) Enforced navigation with 'browse' problems.

6.4.1   Materials

The material used was 'Hypertext on Hypertext' published as a special section of the July 1988 Communications of the ACM, and featuring papers form the Hypertext'87 conference. We used the Hyperties version produced by Ben Shneiderman and his team at the HCI Laboratory, University of Maryland .

Questions designed to encourage a querying approach were as follows:

Q1. How many times does the word 'tailorability' occur?

Q2. What is the title of the Conklin article published in 1987?

Q3. What are the four basic components of hypertext/hypermedia according
to *the article by Halasz?*

Q4. Who is Ben Shneiderman?

Questions designed to encourage a browsing approach were as follows:

B1. Estimate about how many links there are between pages of text in the whole system.

B2. What are the major characteristics of hypertext/hypermedia?

B3. Choose four sentences from the text that best capture the essence of hypertext/hypermedia.

B4. What are the main advantages of using hypertext/hypermedia?

6.4.2 Subjects and Method

Our subjects were 16 Computer Science undergraduate students working on projects at the Institute of Systems Science, Singapore. Although all were computer scientists, none were specialists in the field of hypermedia or information retrieval.

Each of the subjects completed all four problems of each type and encountered enforced query ("Please follow the links to answer the following questions") and enforced mediated search ("Please search for the following") problems. So subjects were aware of the structural responsibility aspect of the task, but not of the two problem types to which they were exposed. Order of administration of problem and search conditions were counterbalanced across subjects to control order effects, each subject attempting two problems for each of our four experimental conditions according to a within-subjects experimental design.

The main dependent variable was the time taken to complete a problem, or abandon a problem. A secondary measure was subjects' ratings of how difficult they found locating a particular solution under the various conditions.

6.4.3   Results

The ratings indicated that subjects generally found the 'browse-encouraging' questions more difficult than the 'query-encouraging' questions whichever strategy was used to try and find an answer. This was confirmed by the timing data from the subjects, where query questions were generally solved significantly more quickly than were browse questions (F[1,15]=4.70, $p< 0.05$).

The data on exploration strategy were less clear-cut, but suggested that mediated search is efficient and popular for solving not only specific (query) problems, but also for more general exploration (browsing) to extract the information needed to arrive at more interpretive types of answer. On average, navigation was rated as more difficult than searching, and also resulted in longer completion times, although these effects only approached significance for completion time scores (F[1,15]=3.22, $p< 0.10$). This may reflect the very high variability in the amount of time different subjects spent on each problem.

Table 6.2 illustrates the completion time results for each problem type and exploration strategy. This illustrates the finding that browse problems were generally more difficult than search problems, and the suggestion that searching is more effective than navigation for both types of problem.

| | Question Type | | |
Strategy	Browse	Query	Both
Navigate	1172 s	950 s	1061 s
Search	1063 s	496 s	779 s
Both	11187s	723 s	

Table 6.2 - Browsing v. searching for two problem types (mean problem solving time)

6.4.4   Discussion

There are problems in carrying out controlled studies that contrast different information exploration strategies. In the first place, there is something intrinsically paradoxical about setting 'browse-encouraging' problems and then taking success as the speed with which an answer could be found. Recall the definition of 'browse' cited earlier: "If you browse you look at several things ... in a casual, unhurried way, in the hope that you might find something interesting" (COBUILD, 1987). Insofar as browsing is, by definition, unhurried, a successful browsing session would be indicated by long completion times, not short as our study assumed. Nor would success be judged by whether a particular answer was found, but rather by what interesting items were found along the way.

This points to a fundamental problem with assessing which information exploration strategies are best for browsing. Our results suggest that mediated search is more effective than navigation in finding answers to two types of problem (though it should be stressed that only the effect of problem type was significant). But it seems likely that neither of these problem types could be said to elicit true browsing behaviour, since we have defined browsing under our model as exploration with no definite target in mind.

In this study we forced users to either navigate or use mediated search. In this situation, and with particular questions to answer, navigation appears to have no advantages for either problem type. This suggests that the strong emphasis on navigation found in the hypermedia literature may be inappropriate. We do suspect, however, that navigation may have advantages not identified by our small study. Users needing to gain an overview of a subject area, or wishing to take advantage of serendipitous discovery, might be cases in point. Even so, it is not certain that these aims can best be achieved through navigation. Non-navigable structural overviews, and a degree of random selection of contents for display, might achieve these two aims, but further experimentation is needed to resolve this issue. It seems pretty clear, though, that any information exploration system should provide mediated search in addition to navigation, if users are ever going to want to access specific items of information.

Further studies are required to tap different aspects of information exploration behaviour, especially in relation to loosely formulated informational needs. More data on user satisfaction with different approaches to exploration would be valuable here.

Additionally, instead of comparing the situation where users may either search or navigate, we need to develop hybrid systems that combine or merge the two in various ways, and then compare user performance and satisfaction in a wider variety of exploration situations.

6.5 DEVELOPING INFORMATION EXPLORATION SYSTEMS

In this section we expand on our taxonomic model by considering directions for the development of practical systems that integrate desirable features for information exploration. We have already pointed to the need for systems which combine traditional information retrieval capabilities with the flexible linking characteristics of hypermedia. We develop this theme in three ways. Firstly, we suggest that extending the notion of a hypermedia link will provide the necessary additional structure to support navigational querying behaviour. Secondly, we re-emphasize the view that mediated search should be integrated into the hypermedia paradigm. Index linking is proposed as a way of avoiding the heavy reliance on descriptive interaction that might be expected from this integration. Finally, we focus on patterns of behaviour that would typify various aspects of the information explorer's task.

6.5.1 Hypermedia and Information Retrieval

One of the dilemmas for hypermedia enthusiasts is how to promote hypermedia as a general information seeking environment. For historical reasons, perhaps, hypermedia has developed as a counterpoint, rather than a complement, to mainstream information retrieval. Thus, while conventional information retrieval systems have used mediated querying, hypermedia developers have emphasized navigational browsing (Figure 6.2). How can our conceptualization of hypermedia and information retrieval be extended to provide more general information exploration mechanisms?

In our view, the hypermedia model can be extended to provide mediated search and querying capabilities, if we extend our view of what a hypermedia link is and how it functions.

The most frequently used hypermedia link is a reference link of the form "Node A refers to Node B." The form of reference is often unspecified, but is assumed to be associative in nature. Unspecified reference links seem to be most appropriate for undirected browsing, which may work for entertainment (e.g., interactive fiction), or even serendipitous learning, but perhaps not for more structured tasks.

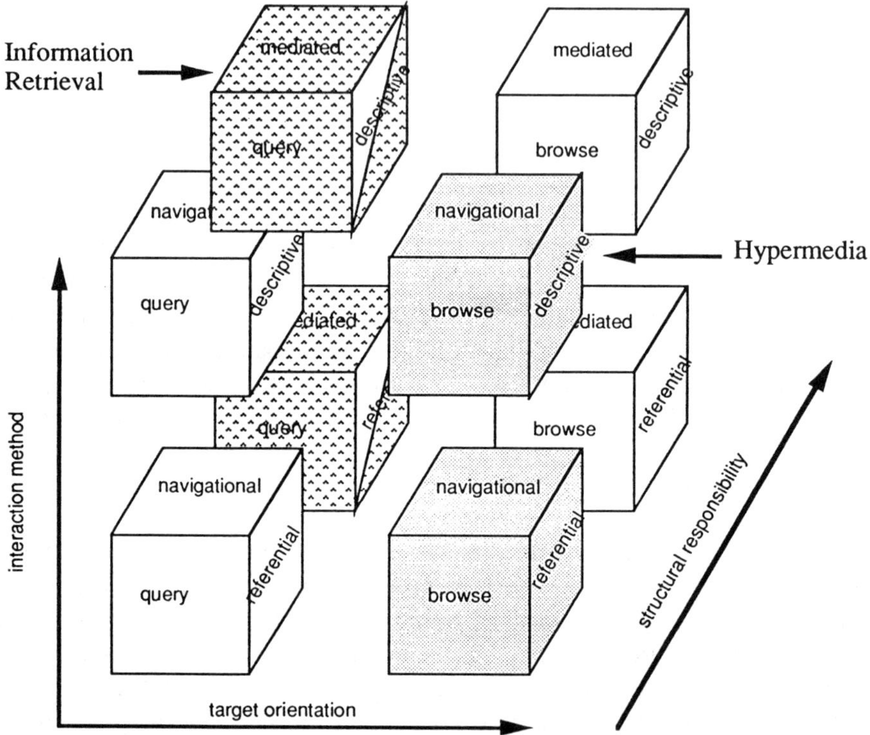

Figure 6.2 - Highlighting information retrieval and hypermedia

Some have looked to a more structured set of reference links as a way of expanding the types of task that hypermedia can handle. Various link types may be used to promote structure such as paths and hierarchical links. Figure 6.3 (after Parsaye *et al.*, 1989) shows three embedded representational structures that may be used for different tasks, or different aspects of the same task. The linear path is useful for following a line of reasoning, while the network provides a browsing capability and the hierarchy provides an index structure and allows the user to explore categorical relationships.

Additional structure might be achieved by seeing hypermedia as a more general knowledge representation environment (Chignell *et al.* 1991). Here the hypermedia would have the type of linking representative of concepts and their interrelations that has been used in the semantic network approach to knowledge representation (e.g. Norman and Rumelhart, 1975).

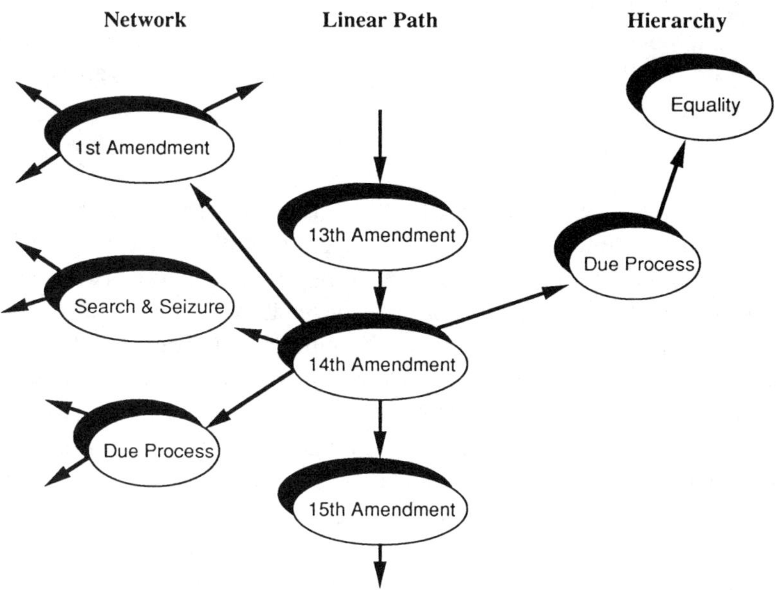

Figure 6.3 - Types of organizational structuring

The structure provided by these sophisticated linking techniques may permit a style of navigational querying where the user traverses links to find specific information (as in the Renaissance article discussed above). However, even in this style of interaction there appears to be a need for an entry point into the hypermedia. Some developers have got around this problem by simply defining a start-up node or "gateway" that is the same for all users at all times. Often this gateway node is actually a "welcome screen" which then leads into a menu.

Command menus can be thought of as a compromise between navigational and mediated search. Here the choice element of referential selection (usually reserved for navigation) is preserved, but the effect of choice is to implement a descriptive command, similar to those that are written in mediated search. Non-hierarchical menus that contain lists of alternative topics provide a presentation style that facilitates information exploration by partitioning the available navigation choices from the nodes in which they occur. Thus menus tend to serve as signposts in hypermedia, and as bridges between navigation and mediated search.

The use of menus in a combined model of information exploration is one of the most challenging aspects of integrating hypermedia and information retrieval. Shneiderman (1987b) has used the term embedded menu to describe the use of highlighted text to denote the available links within a hypermedia node. These embedded links can of course be shown as highlighted icons in a graphical display. However, we would like to distinguish here between what we shall refer to as intrinsic menus and extrinsic menus.

Intrinsic menus point to related information based on the content of the current node. In contrast, extrinsic menus tend to point to topics (usually related to or following on from the current node topic) that exist as other nodes in the hypermedia. Thus extrinsic menus supplement the signalling in intrinsic menus and reference links by providing more general access to topics within hypermedia. Topics within an extrinsic menu may vary in relatedness from being closely related (reference-linked) to topics in the current node to being almost totally unrelated. In the latter case, the unrelated menu items may serve as convenient access points to general regions or topics in the hypermedia, thereby breaking the "tyranny of the reference link." These unrelated menu items are then functionally equivalent to a mediated search on the topic that they represent. The selection of such a menu item might lead directly to the most salient node on that topic, or it might lead to a set of nodes on that topic being retrieved, which can then be browsed in some fashion.

Expanding the reference link to include a more general knowledge representation function, along with using extrinsic menus to improve access within hypermedia, can obviously assist navigation. Extrinsic menus also provide a convenient way of merging mediated search and navigation. However, basic navigation necessarily is a "link by link" process. This type of process is inefficient if the user has some information target in mind, and more conventional mediated querying is available. This may explain why searching for information in a linear fashion is often preferred to navigating hypermedia by link traversal (e.g. McKnight *et al.*, 1989; Monk *et al.*, 1988).

6.5.2 Index Linking

Another approach to making hypermedia more usable is to incorporate mediated search into the hypermedia paradigm (Frisse, 1988; Wang and Chua, 1990). One strategy for doing this is to index the nodes as if they were documents in a bibliographic information retrieval system. Index-based mediated search may then be used to access relevant nodes in the hypermedia. However, the descriptive style of interaction used in Boolean search systems and relational databases has been shown to be difficult for many users. Is it possible then to define a more usable style of mediated search that provides appropriate topic access starting points? Our solution to this problem is to propose an 'index linking' process, as described below.

We assume that the nodes in the hypermedia system are described by a set of index terms. These index terms may be used as the basis for automatic linking, but here we will focus on their use for information exploration in an existing hypermedia document. We can imagine the index as a separate entity that is connected to the hypermedia by 'index links' that emanate from each node to the terms in the index that it is indexed by. The important point to note in the index linking model is that mediated search is launched from inside the hypermedia rather than being launched from outside the information as is generally the case in information retrieval.

Thus, the user may be at a node, and he spots an index link that appears relevant. He may now move to the index via that link. On reading the content of that index node and determining that it is relevant he may then add it to his 'hypermedia query'. At this point, all the nodes that are indexed by that term are assigned a higher weight (made relatively more accessible), as they would be in other information retrieval systems. In index linking though, the index itself is organized as navigable hypermedia. Thus the user may trigger mediated search by browsing through the index and marking index nodes that appear to be relevant. In other words, he has achieved what is normally attempted through descriptive interaction (which can be problematic for the non-specialist), by means of referential interaction.

An index term may be an aggregate that explains the use of the term in different contexts. For instance the term mercury may explain its use in different contexts (the name of a planet, an element of the periodic table, etc.). The user may then select the index term within one of more of these contexts. This type of context selection and restriction serves some of the functionality of the NOT operator in Boolean querying.

Working within the index, the user sets up weightings that will then apply in the hypermedia. Restriction of context is handled by selection from within aggregated index nodes. At this point the index weighting functions as an additive linear model. However, the user may at any point return to the hypermedia either by returning to one of the nodes previously visited or by moving to one of the highly weighted nodes based on the current selection of nodes within the index. Once within the hypermedia, the user may refine the query by providing relevance feedback of two types. Firstly, through the act of link traversal, nodes visited will have the weightings of their index terms boosted. Second, by operating on the index terms directly, individual terms will be flagged as relevant (this can happen within a hypermedia node or within the index).

Our description of index linking makes no commitment to a particular style of user feedback. There are a number of ways in which user feedback might modify term weights and link availability. For instance, relevance feedback and term weighting methods might be used (Salton, 1989) or, more speculatively, Bayesian updating of belief, or connectionist models (Frisse, 1988, p. 884).

Given an appropriate method of user feedback, index linking is a model for combining navigation and mediated search into an integrated paradigm. With index linking the navigational style of movement between nodes is preserved, but there is also the possibility of mediated search and of an interesting form of constrained navigation where the nature of the current query limits navigational choices while the act of navigation itself modifies the currently defined query.

Ideally, information exploration strategies should be implemented in an environment where smooth transitions between browsing and querying, and between navigation and mediated search are possible. Index linking appears to be a useful strategy for making this possible. An initial approach in this direction has been described by Thompson and Croft (1989). Their I^3R system contains a model of the information seeking process involving three main steps:

- characterizing the user (e.g., expert or novice)
- characterizing the information need
- searching for relevant documents

The search for relevant documents then consists of a search for documents, followed by an evaluation phase which may in turn be followed by a further search. Within the search process itself, users may build queries directly or may paste together query phrases based on words extracted from documents within the system. In addition, users may search by concepts (index terms) as well as by documents. One of the interesting features of the I3R system is that it is organized as a blackboard system, with a number of "experts" including a control expert, a user model builder, a domain knowledge expert, and a browsing expert. However, smooth integration between browsing and querying is not yet available in current information retrieval or hypertext systems.

6.5.3 Patterns of Exploration Behaviour

The model of information exploration we have presented is based on a logical analysis of the information seeking operations possible in information retrieval systems and hypertext. However, the effectiveness of an information exploration system is ultimately determined by the behavioural patterns adopted by its users. As we have suggested, exploration should be a flexible combination of browsing and querying, navigation and mediated searching; the point of such combinations, and the basis for the design of exploratory systems, is the information exploration behaviours that can be supported. In this section we expand on our taxonomic model of the dimensions of exploration by considering in more detail various exploration behaviours in relation to that model, drawing heavily on the work of Ellis (1989).

Based on extensive interviews with social science researchers, Ellis (1989) found evidence for a behavioural model of information seeking. Ellis's study was influenced by the fact that it was conducted with researchers who used conventional (i.e. non-hypertext) information retrieval systems. Thus the findings may underestimate the amount of browsing that would occur in a more balanced information exploration environment that included both browsing and querying capabilities. Even so, the component information seeking processes proposed by Ellis appear to be highly compatible with the general model of information exploration described in this paper.

Ellis's model of information seeking encompasses six component activities:

- Starting
- Chaining
- Browsing
- Differentiation
- Monitoring
- Extracting

6.5.3.1 Starting

Starting is a process of looking for key references or expert guidance that can provide the right orientation to a search. According to Ellis, starting might involve discussion of a list of possible search terms with an expert, or identification of a book or article that is particularly relevant and a good starting point for the exploration.

From our perspective, we can contrast starting with a query versus starting with a browse. In a querying style of search starting involves formulating the search target or topic. In a more browsing style of search this involves identifying the starting point for the search (i.e. the initial context for browsing). The starting process might consist of menu-based selection of a start node, followed by browsing of hypertext to get a sense of the topic of interest.

6.5.3.2 Chaining

Chaining consists of following referential connection between material. Obviously navigation through sequences of hypertext links is somewhat analogous to chaining. However in chaining the user tends to follow a sequence of links of a particular kind. For instance, a form of chaining can be achieved using citation indices, where one can either move backward from one text to a document that is cited within it, or forward from a citation to the texts that cite it. In either case the user traverses a chain of citation links.

The distinction between forward and backward chaining during information exploration is also applicable in navigation through a hypertext that contains asymmetric links (where one moves backward by finding the nodes that have links to the current node). We shall refer to the navigation process where a variety of link types are used as "linking" to distinguish it from link specific types of "chaining."

6.5.3.3 Differentiation

In browsing and querying, differences between sources of information may be used as filters on the nature and quality of the material examined, or to restrict the context so that only relevant information is made available. Ellis refers to this process as differentiation. For instance, certain authors, publishers, or journals are usually more highly regarded in a topic area, and thus are given more attention during information exploration. In mediated search, differentiation can be achieved by restricting the search to certain databases, and in browsing by highlighting nodes that have been created by highly regarded authors or that have been extracted from particular sources.

6.5.3.4 Monitoring

Users may also wish to maintain awareness of developments in a field through the monitoring of particular sources. In a general information exploration environment that is updated over time, users should be able to review the new information that is relevant to their interests. One way to do this is to maintain a profile of the user's interest. New information that matches this profile is then passed on to the user. In mediated search systems this profile consists of a query and new documents are matched against this query. Since monitoring implies that the user has a target in mind, it is applicable to querying rather than browsing. A navigational approach to monitoring is, however, possible. Nodes that are new or that have not been previously visited by the user may be highlighted. Navigational monitoring would then consist of navigating through the new information in the network from time to time.

6.5.3.5 Extracting and Evaluating

Extracting, where the user reads through the information source to find material of interest, is the final behavioural component of Ellis's model. Extraction is a major problem with information retrieval systems that only contain abstracts or titles. The user must locate the hard copy of the original source which in some cases may take considerable time. In contrast, extraction is an integral part of hypertext navigation, since the contents of the current node may be viewed in their entirety.

One vital additional behaviour to consider is evaluation. Through evaluating outcomes, the user determines the quality of the information found and the effectiveness of the retrieval strategy (including the index terms if mediated search is being used). For instance, relevance feedback may be used to modify a query based on the user's evaluation of mediated retrieval. Evaluation may also occur during navigation, although it may not be public or observable in terms of selection of documents or explicit modification of a query. After reaching a node a user may decide that it is not leading in a promising direction and backtrack to a prior node, or the user may find that a particular type of link tends to lead to more interesting nodes and start "chaining" along that type of link.

6.5.3.6 Target Specificity

A major distinction in our model is between querying and browsing, distinguished by the degree of target specificity in the mind of the user. From a behavioural point of view, the starting point of querying is target identification, while browsing begins with a starting context which is typically much less specific (e.g. go to the table of contents of the encyclopaedia and look for an interesting topic).

Figure 6.4 provides a visual description of the information exploration behaviours we have considered above, in relation to the distinction between browsing and querying. This complements the static model of the dimensions of information exploration that we showed in Figure 6.1.

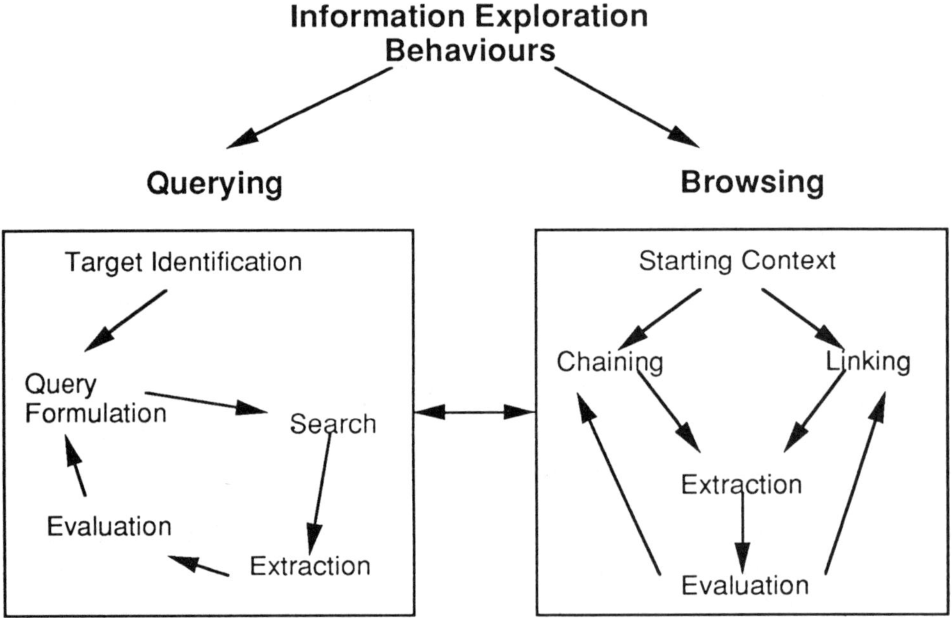

Figure 6.4 - Information exploration behaviour patterns

In querying, target identification is followed by one or more cycles of query formulation, search, extraction, and evaluation. For browsing, selection of the starting context is followed by either chaining or linking and then by extraction, evaluation and further chaining or linking. The double-headed arrow between querying and browsing in the figure indicates that during information exploration users should be able to switch strategies without too much difficulty.

6.6   CONCLUSIONS

Our three dimensional model provides a focus for empirically testing hypermedia information retrieval tools in relation to task needs. Similarly, the model provides an approach to testing the closely related questions of how information can best be structured for different tasks, and of how different structures can best be conveyed to users and navigated by them. Some directions for future empirical research on these usability issues are described elsewhere in the book (Chapter 4).

We believe that it is possible to develop systems that capture all three of our dimensions of information exploration. As an initial step, a concept-based hypermedia system with mediated search could be developed. A prototype hypermedia system along these lines has already been developed at the Institute of Systems Science (Wang and Chua, 1990; Chua and Lai, 1991).

However, the fact that systems can be defined which merge querying with browsing and navigation with mediated search says little about how they should be built in order to enhance usability and information exploration effectiveness. Adding new capabilities for information exploration may not always make users more productive. For instance, after several years of development hypermedia systems have yet to prove themselves clearly superior over linear text in a broad range of tasks. If anything linear text appears to have fared better in the few comparisons that have been carried out.

Much more human factors research is needed to determine how integrated information exploration systems should be constructed. We know very little about how people will explore information if tools that combine the features of hypermedia and of traditional information retrieval are available. This is not surprising since analogous tools have not previously been available. However, even in the absence of such tools types of exploration behaviour can be observed and classified. For instance, researchers carry out browsing in non-hypertext environments by looking through tables of contents of books, abstracting journals such as Current Contents, or by simply browsing through library stacks. More work is needed to identify the larger patterns of exploration that achieve users' task goals.

Education is one application area where the need to blend various ways of interacting with information sources in different media is particularly obvious. Currently, our knowledge is inadequate to characterize how different types of system should be designed to meet varying educational targets. The problem is a complex one, involving interactions between not only our three dimensions of interaction, but also such factors as educational objectives, pedagogic approach, and the type of cognitive effort required, as well as the system image chosen - whether this be based around some overall metaphor or other conceptual model (as discussed in earlier chapters). Some of these many elements are portrayed in Figure 6.5, below, with possible linkages between elements tentatively sketched in.

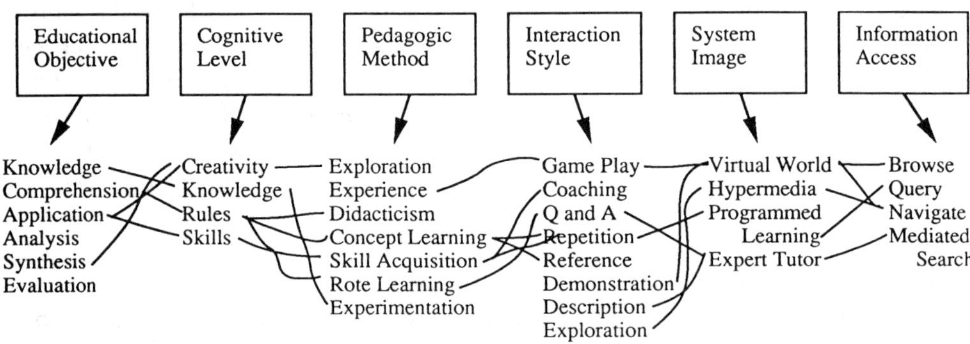

Figure 6.5 - Aspects of learning and teaching by computer

The failure of users to adapt to the Boolean querying requirement of many information retrieval systems stands as an instructive reminder of the need to craft information technologies to match the capabilities and requirements of the human user. The index linking approach introduced above promotes a hybrid form of exploration that includes a simpler style of querying that complements navigational browsing.

We predict that hybrid forms of exploration will increase in popularity as hypermedia and information retrieval systems become more sophisticated and sensitive to users' varied task requirements. We have attempted to represent the universe of interactive possibilities from which these hybrids will be designed. However, development of future information systems should be constrained by logical and behavioural analysis of information exploration. Based on the existing empirical evidence and our model of information exploration, we make the following recommendations.

If users know exactly what they are looking for (i.e. they are querying) then following links is not an effective way of finding the information and good mediated retrieval is needed. In addition, structuring, such as the use of menu hierarchies, will help narrow down the topics of interest.

If users do not know exactly what they are looking for (i.e. they are browsing) then following linear sequences is more efficient than jumping around. Structuring may also help, but there is a flexibility trade-off where structure may "channel" the search and restrict the breadth of exploration. If the user has at least a rough idea of the topic of interest, mediated retrieval may help narrow down the area of exploration.

We can identify two major trends in information exploration systems, which may be referred to as "expertext" and "pilotext." In practice, actual systems should consist of collections of features that can be mixed and matched according to the application needs.

Expertext is implicit hypermedia containing rules to aid information selection (through the use of conditional links), structure that is hidden from user (with an emphasis on mediated information retrieval), and associated text and media that are used to explain advice. Expertext would typically be aimed at consultative or intelligent tutoring system applications. Expertext and its advantages are reviewed by Rada and Barlow (1988).

Pilotext is explicit hypermedia featuring user-initiated navigation (although 'autopilots' may be used too), sophisticated structural models and browse tools (because of an emphasis on navigation). The target applications for pilotext tend to be explorational, such as education, reference and publicly accessed information.

Expertext, pilotext, and related technologies such as hybrid information systems may well revolutionize the ways in which people carry out information exploration. However, programmatic research is needed to determine what functionalities and structures will be most useful for information exploration.

Chapter 7

Usability Assessment: Two Case Studies

"Multimedia interfaces are not just about extending the choice of media available, more importantly they are about improving interfaces to computers by improving the communication bandwidth in such a manner that human beings will find themselves in an advantageous position."

James L Alty (1991)

7.1   INTRODUCTION

This chapter presents two case studies of usability assessment for multimedia systems. The two are quite different both in the approach taken and in the aims of the evaluations. In the first case, a complete Computer-Aided Instruction (CAI) package was assessed for a client interested in the development of training systems for the assimilation of practical skills - skills that are very closely tied to real life tasks where fast and correct responses are absolutely vital. Therefore the method of assessment had to address this requirement. The approach adopted was a combination of scenario-based tests, students' attitude evaluation, and expert assessment of the CAI program features.

In the second case, the aim was rather different. Here a technique for generating hypermedia semi-automatically from existing, traditional materials was the subject of the evaluation. As we have already seen in earlier chapters, the success of a hypermedia system depends crucially on the appropriateness of the presentation of material as chunks of information (nodes) and their interconnections (links). What was required from this evaluation was not a global assessment of a complete CAI package as in the first case, but rather an analytic technique for assessing the success or otherwise of the semi-automatic "hypertization" process, in particular, how the results of the linking approach compared with that of manually authored hypermedia.

7.2 ASSESSMENT OF A COMPLETE CAI PACKAGE

The approach taken to providing this evaluation included a description of the system, a statement of the aims of the assessment, a description of the method used, a detailed account of the results obtained, and conclusions and recommendations for further development of the software. These are presented below (in edited form) to give the reader an insight into the outcome of the evaluation process - a report on the software and its usability as provided to a client responsible for developing such a training system.

7.2.1 Description of the Software

The software was designed to provide students with experience in leading a military operation, to supplement the theoretical instruction and practical training in the field they currently experience. The approach of the training is to allow a 'free play' style of interaction, stressing an experiential mode of learning. To this end the software includes terrain images - stills taken off video - of a physical location, combined with maps and other tools that simulate the resources and experiences of a leader in the field. The tools providing access to information are presented to the student in the form of buttons and menus. The planning phase is crucial and represents the major elements of what is taught. A plan editor is available for plan formulation and specification. An intelligent tutor module evaluates the student's plan and suggests improvements, though the student need not adopt these suggestions. Once the plan is complete the operational simulation phase begins. Here the student sees the outcome of his plan directly; the student learns by his mistakes and continues in this manner until he comes up with a successful plan. An additional tutorial module contains the basic facts that a student would learn in a classroom lesson on the topic. Students may work their way through the tutorial before using the simulation, and may also access tutorial information at any time during a session. There are currently no time constraints placed on the students during their interactions with the system, but the tutoring policy is to move students forward if they are making slow progress.

The main aim of the software is to improve the quality of training on a particular military operation. Because of practical constraints, not all students are given experience with leading this operation in the field. Typically, more than half of any group of students only participate in a non-leadership role. It is expected that putting all members of a section in the role of commander, through interacting with the simulation program, will significantly enhance the general level of competence of the section on this topic and will be a better preparation for each student's future role as leader than is currently provided. Thus, the aim is to improve quality rather than, for example, reduce the time spent on training this component as compared to current practice.

7.2.2 Aims of the Evaluation

Given the objectives of the software I aim, in this evaluation, to assess the extent to which using the program improves students' performance and knowledge of what is involved in leading this operation.

Another aim is to provide feedback on the design of the various components of the application, and make suggestions for improvements as necessary. In this report, comments are provided on:

- the tutorial module
- the help module
- presentation of information, information tools and feedback
- the planning and tutoring components
- the user interface in general

General recommendations on user interface aspects of future CAI programs are also made. My overall objective is to provide information to guide future work on the design of CAI software for this organization.

7.2.3 Practical Constraints on Timing and Approach

For a valid test of the effectiveness of the software to be carried out, it is necessary to compare students who have experienced the training against otherwise similar students who have not. It was planned for 3 out of an intake of 36 sections to take the CAI course. Since only a few students from each section would be assessed for leadership in the field, field performance (as judged by instructors) could only be used as a measure for these users of the CAI package, which would be insufficient for firm conclusions to be drawn from the results without further evidence. One way of increasing these numbers would be to select only those students that were to experience leadership in the field as the students of the CAI course. But it is very important not to treat the test group any differently from the rest of the intake, except for their exposure to the software to be assessed. Selecting all leaders would certainly interfere with group dynamics and would tend to produce a 'halo effect' - the selected students would see themselves as special and might, for this reason alone, be motivated to perform better than their peers who were not so selected. For this reason it was decided to develop a written test that would effectively assess both theoretical knowledge and practical skills, the latter through answering questions based on scenario descriptions of relevant situations.

The timing of the evaluation was dependent on the training programme schedule for students. Our plan was designed to fit in with this schedule, but delays in this schedule inevitably led to delay in the completion of the evaluation.

7.2.4   Evaluation Method

7.2.4.1 Introduction

This evaluation provides feedback on the software and suggestions for CAI design in the future. It is therefore a formative evaluation, not a summative evaluation. Summative evaluations generally represent the final assessment of whether or not an operational system should be adopted. This decision is usually taken by management through a consideration of costs against benefits. In contrast, formative evaluations have the main purpose of improving prototype instructional systems. They use as their principal source of data the actual performance of students, and they are assessed by an instructional or human factors specialist (or both).

The software was examined in three main ways:

> (i) through an assessment of students' performance, by administering a specially designed test, comparing students who had used the program with those who had not,

> (ii) by canvassing the subjective opinions of students and instructors about the program by means of a specially designed questionnaire,

> (iii) through 'expert assessment' of the software.

This multi-faceted approach ensures that a broad view is taken during the evaluation, and provides a suitable basis for recommendations about future CAI work.

7.2.4.2   Assessment of Students' Performance

Altogether, six sets of realistic scenarios were devised. These made use of terrain photographs and maps to describe an operational problem. Students were required solve problems based on these scenarios, using paper and pencil. They also attempted to complete a set of questions tapping retained knowledge about this type of operation, but not based on specific situations. During assessment, each student completed two of the six scenario problems. The selection and ordering of these problems was controlled so that no student ever encountered the same problem twice and each problem was equally exposed in each group to be assessed.

Students who had used the program were compared with others who had not. Students who used the program were assessed before and after use. This allows us to look at the effect of using the program on students' performance, and to compare this with the performance of students trained in more conventional ways.

7.2.4.3   Assessment of Students' and Instructors' Attitudes

Students and instructors who are familiar with the system were asked to complete a questionnaire aimed at eliciting their views of the software in terms of its effectiveness, the level of interest in use, duration of a training session, design aspects of the presentation, ease of use, clarity of instructions, comparison with other methods of instruction, and overall subjective rating. The questionnaires used are given in Appendix 1 at the end of the chapter, which provides a summary of the ratings from the first trial (for students only, although instructors also completed the questionnaire).

7.2.4.4   Expert Assessment of Software

Expert assessment covered all of the significant user-related modules of the training software:

- the tutorial module
- the help module
- the planning, tutor components and simulation
- presentation of information, information tools and feedback
- the user interface in general.

However, it is important also to view the software from the user's perspective, as a complete, integrated, instructional experience.

The package was evaluated in terms of the following criteria:

- quality of instruction methods and guidance
- quality of design
- quality of program
- quality of training content.

7.2.4.5 Quality of Instruction Methods and Guidance

This refers to the extent to which the instruction method adopted is suited to the objectives of the training, and whether the necessary information and guidance is provided appropriately. Issues include whether it is easy for students to follow what is going on in the training, know what to do when action is required from them, control their interactions with the system, and know how to obtain guidance when necessary. The quality of any text used for guidance or instruction is important; it should be clear, concise, and unambiguous. The overall logic of the training approach, in terms of the sequence of events encountered by students, was examined, including the level of efficiency/redundancy, relative emphases on sub-topics, student involvement, and pace.

7.2.4.6 Quality of Design

Quality of design covers the cosmetic aspects of the package, such as the screen layout, use of space, presentation of information, and use of colour, sound and animation. Any undesirable peculiarities, errors, or inconsistencies in the way material is presented on the screen were noted. The overall appeal of design was also assessed; this is a rather subjective matter but it is useful to have feedback from assessors who were not themselves involved in the design.

7.2.4.7 Quality of Program

The program may have problems in terms of correctness of execution which have remained undetected during the debugging phase of implementation. These are likely to be uncommon, and unlikely to cause a program crash. It is quite easy for the programming team to miss a few of these kinds of errors. Evaluators may identify these program logic faults if they spend a reasonable amount of time using the system in the role of students. All possible student inputs, including a realistic range of legal entries, should be catered for.

7.2.4.8 Quality of Training Content

This category of evaluation most directly addresses the coverage of material provided by the training program, as compared with other methods of instruction. If a training system is going to be used successfully, it clearly must cover the material it addresses to a level of detail that is acceptable to all concerned in the training process. It would be possible to have a training package that was excellent in terms of instruction, design, and program, but which simply covered too much or too little material for the purpose for which it was intended. It is also important to consider whether the package is likely to fit in with, or lead on to, training on related topics. Expert evaluation in this category supplements the ratings to be elicited from students and trainers.

7.2.5   Summary Evaluation and Design Recommendations

The results obtained from the various stages of the evaluation are reported in section 7.3. From these an overall summary evaluation of the software has been produced (section 7.4). Conclusions were drawn from the assessment of students' performance about the effectiveness of the program as a method of training students on this operation and how this method compares with classroom training and practical experience in the field. Students' and instructors' attitude evaluation allows conclusions about the subjective acceptability of the program to be drawn, and may also throw up aspects of the system not identified by the other tests. It is important to assess subjective acceptability since a program that is not well received by its users is unlikely to be successful in the long run, however good it may appear to be on other criteria. The expert assessment was more fine-grained and analytical. It provides the basis for design recommendations for improving the current package and more general guidelines that will be applicable to the production of other educational software in the future.

7.3 RESULTS OF CAI PACKAGE EVALUATION

7.3.1 Introduction: two trials

The CAI program was tested in two separate trials. In the first, eight students participated in each of two groups, the control group and the test group, making 16 students in all. The test group were those students who experienced the software, while the control group provided a basis for the comparison of performance. Both groups had already undergone training via lectures and in the field. The test group answered the scenario questions before experiencing the software and again afterwards. The control group answered the questions on one occasion only. At each evaluation session, each student completed questions on two out of the six scenarios that were prepared. Scores for the pre- and post-test groups were compared to assess the extra value accruing from the use of the software. Each of these scores were also compared with the performance of the control group. It was expected that the control and pre-test scores would not be different from each other, and that the post-test scores would be significantly higher than either. Test group students also filled out the Student Attitude Questionnaires (see Appendix 1) after using the software. These questionnaires were also filled out by four instructors.

The second trial was generally similar to the first, but more comprehensive. Sixteen students were allocated to each of two conditions, test (who experienced the software) and control (who did not). Both groups were tested on scenario questions twice. In the first, both groups ('pre-CAI' and 'pre-control' scores) had experienced a classroom lecture on 'Appreciation of Situation' but had not had any other training on the target operation. In the second, both groups had experienced lectures and field training. The test group ('post-CAI' scores) had also experienced the software, whereas the control group ('post-control' scores) had not. It was expected that the group that had used the software would gain the highest scores, which would be better than all other scores. The post-control group was expected to yield higher scores than the pre-CAI and pre-control groups, while these latter two groups would not be different from each other. The post-test group also completed the Student Attitude Questionnaire.

7.3.2 Assessment of Performance with Scenario Questions

7.3.2.1 First Trial

Sixteen students took part in the first trial. Eight of them comprised a control group who did not experience using the software. The other eight were tested on two of the scenarios before using the software, and again on two different scenarios after using the system. Scores on the test were as follows:

Control group:	12.6 (average number of correct answers out of 25)
Pre-CAI group:	11.6
Post-CAI group:	16.5

Statistical analysis showed that the difference between the pre- and post-CAI groups (actually the same eight students) was very significant ($p< .001$), and the difference between the post-CAI group and the control group was also significant ($p< .01$). There was no significant difference between the pre-CAI group and the control group. In other words, the control group and the pre-CAI group scored to a similar level as would be expected, but the post-CAI group performed significantly better than both of them. This finding supports the hypothesis that use of the software results in a significant improvement in knowledge about the operation, as assessed by the scenario questions.

7.3.2.2 Second Trial

The second trial was a little more comprehensive than the first, although the same scenario assessment method was used. Sixteen students comprised a control group that was tested before and after field training (they did not experience the software). Another 16 students comprised the test group and were assessed before and after using the software. Scores were as follows:

Pre-control group:	13.1 (average number of correct answers out of 25)
Post-control group:	14.1
Pre-CAI group:	13.5
Post-CAI group:	14.8

Statistical analysis showed that the performance of the pre-CAI and pre-control groups did not differ significantly. Performance of the post-CAI group was again significantly better than the pre-CAI group ($p< .01$) and also better than than the pre-control group ($p < .005$). The post-control group performed significantly better than the pre-control group ($p < .01$). There was no difference in performance between the post-CAI group and the post-control group.

7.3.3   Results from Student Attitude Questionnaire

7.3.3.1 First Trial

Eight students and 4 instructors completed these questionnaires.
Student responses were as follows:

Overall, the ratings were positive (mean rating on a 5-point scale = 3.7). Questionnaire responses were in terms of eight categories of question:

Personal affect	= 3.8
Systematic arrangement	= 3.9
Task relevance	= 3.9
Understandability	= 3.8
Components	= 3.0
Credibility	= 3.9
Suitability	= 3.7
Workload	= 3.7

This suggests that the system was well designed for the selected task in terms of almost all of these aspects.

Refer to Appendix 1 for details of the questions used and specific responses obtained. The relatively low rating for 'Components' is mostly due to the rated low usage (between 'Not Often' and 'Never') of the tutorial component (question 15), and also to an overall 'Don't Know' response to whether users felt in control (question 17).

All other questions elicited a positive rating when scores were averaged across individuals. Particularly positive ratings were elicited by question 1 (how interesting?), question 5 (like to use again?), question 7 (should these systems be used for military training?), question 11 (this training helpful in field?), question 13 (easy to understand?), question 20 (could you rely on what you have learned?), question 26 (feel under time pressure?) and question 27 (were you relaxed or tense?).

These results suggest that the students found the system interesting, enjoyable and useful. There is no indication of any usability or credibility problems arising from the current design.

Instructor Responses were as follows:

Overall, the ratings were again positive, though less so than with students (mean rating on a 5-point scale = 3.3). The results for each category were as follows:

Personal affect	= 2.9
Systematic arrangement	= 3.3
Task relevance	= 3.5
Understandability	= 3.5
Components	= 3.0
Credibility	= 3.6
Suitability	= 3.5
Workload	= 3.7

Responses to personal affect questions were noticeably less favourable than those of the students, perhaps reflecting the instructors' high level of familiarity with the presented material. There was no indication from their responses of any problems in the design of the system.

Interestingly, all four instructors were unhappy with their own performance with the system (question 4). Instructors seldom or never used the tutorial component. Unlike students, instructors tended to rate the completeness of the training rather poorly (question 23). They also found the system more complicated than did students (question 25).

Particularly positive ratings were elicited by question 11 (helpful in the field?), question 13 (easy to understand?), question 20 (could you rely on what you have learned in the field?), question 21 (was the training relevant?), question 22 (is this training method appropriate?), question 24 (easy to use?), question 26 (did you feel under time pressure?) and question 27 (were you relaxed or tense?).

7.3.3.2 Second Trial

Sixteen students took part in the second trial.

Student responses were as follows:

The pattern of responses was very similar to that of students in the first trial, which serves to validate the results. The overall mean rating of the system on a 5-point scale was 3.8. The results for each category were as follows:

Personal affect	= 3.8
Systematic arrangement	= 4.0
Task relevance	= 3.7
Understandability	= 4.2
Components	= 3.1
Credibility	= 3.6
Suitability	= 4.0
Workload	= 3.9

The relatively low rating which was again obtained for 'Components' was due to low usage of the tutorial component, as in the first trial. The only other question which elicited a low rating was question 4 ('Are you happy with your performance?').

Particularly positive ratings were obtained from question 1 (how interesting?), question 5 (like to use again?), question 7 (should these systems be used for military training?), question 8 (how well organized?), question 13 (how easy to understand?), question 14 (how easy was the written information to follow?), question 23 (how complete?), question 24 (easy or difficult to use?), and question 27 (were you relaxed or tense?).

We can conclude that the users judged the system to be well designed, particularly in terms of understandability, systematic arrangement, and suitability for its purpose.

Several of the students offered useful comments to improve the effectiveness of the system.

7.3.4   Expert Assessment of Program

7.3.4.1 Observations on Software:

Tutorial module

The tutorial module is a passive and self-contained summary of the information upon which the main CAI program is based. It uses text and some simple graphics and animation to convey the main points that students should assimilate during their training on this topic. Students are free to call up the tutorial component at any point from the main program, via the 'Help' pull-down menu. Within the tutorial module there is no questioning of students or feedback on performance, it has a purely reference function.

There are currently two versions of the tutorial, differing mostly in terms of visual layout design. The more recent version has a more modern and elegant appearance but is a little more opaque in terms of providing cues to where the student is in relation to the organization of the information.

On the whole, the design of both versions of the tutorial is good and the presentation is highly consistent within each version. The second version has more minor bugs in the program. Both versions contain a few typographic errors. In the first version, the placement of buttons sometimes partially obscures the associated label. The main control buttons (next, previous, menu, quit) are nicely done, but sometimes appear unnecessarily.

Students used the tutorial before using the main program, but seldom or never referred to it during use of the main program (see section 7.3.3).

Help module

Users accessing help via a pull-down menu from the main screen are offered a choice of either consulting the tutorial (see above) or obtaining guidance from the automatic tutor component. The tutor suggests next action or complete operation plans in response to a request from the user, or when the tutor judges that this is necessary on the basis of the user's behaviour. Generally, the tutor was not explicitly consulted by users but was encountered during the process of planning (see below). It may not be necessary to provide access to the tutor via an explicit request.

Planning, tutor components, and simulation

The tutor is concerned with monitoring and advising on the plan, initially in terms of the sequence of actions selected, then in terms of specific aspects such as the route chosen (cover, direction, distance, etc.). During advice on the sequence of activities some inconsistencies were encountered (examples provided to client). Some of these placed the student in a seemingly inescapable loop. The strategy generally taken in offering advice is to give the next suggested action and indicate that it has already been done. Sometimes this indication was missing, which causes the confusion. It would be better to force the student to take the correct action rather than have the tutor carry it out for him. Leaving the initiative with the student would strengthen the memorization of the correct sequence of activities.

If the student takes too long getting to the detailed planning stage, the tutor will force him to start planning. This is another example of the tutor taking the initiative from the student and will tend to have a bad effect on the student's memory of the actions that should lead up to the planning stage. The advantage of the tutor taking the initiative is that it prevents the student getting stuck at particular stages in the exercise. To increase the student's awareness of the process, however, it might be preferable to leave the initiative with users even though this would mean that progress through the program would be relatively slow, especially in the early stages.

During the planning phase itself, the feedback offered is generally appropriate and helpful and reinforces correct decisions well. The diagnosis of the overall plan offered after an operation was inaccurate at times. Comments such as "Your route crosses the line of fire" or "Your route is mostly exposed to the enemy" sometimes did not match the planned route. After several attempts at planning and receiving negative feedback the tutor will offer an improved plan. This is a good strategy and encourages the student to consider different approaches to an operation that is proving difficult to plan. Diagnosis comments did not always seem to take account of revisions to the plan made by the student. The same negative comments would be made even when a plan had been revised to take account of those comments given earlier. Even when the tutor offered a plan and this was accepted and carried out in a simulated operation, the original negative comments could still be offered, causing considerable confusion.

There seems to be a general problem about revising the tutor's view of the planned operation which results in outdated advice. Occasionally the tutor seemed to have the wrong impression of the location of the operational unit (examples given to client).

The simulated operation, with its 'cartoon' view of the landscape works well and helps visualization of the terrain. However, the use of the 'Continue' button is not ideal and can cause confusion; it might be better to simply automate the animation after selections have been made. When the mission was such that an immediate action was called for, no movement took place during the animation. On one mission the section position was off screen, which made planning impossible.

Presentation of information

The video images at the beginning of a mission are intended to give an all-round view of the location and terrain and add to the realism of the presentation. This is a good idea but the number and quality of images is not sufficient. The views are discontinuous and so the user does not get the impression of scanning round an actual location. One way around this problem is to use a camera fitted with a fish-eye lens and pointed at the sky. This can capture a continuous image where all 360 degrees of the horizon are included. Another alternative is to digitize sequences of motion video that capture the all-round view from selected locations, but this is expensive in memory terms. Currently, the resolution of the video images is also too low.

Although the 'cartoon' presentation of the operation is stylized it is generally effective, though the colours could be improved.

The tutor sometimes offers an improved plan of its own for the student to view. To do so the student must move the message window out of the way. This is inconvenient and not all users will know how to do it. It would be better to have a simple button which would result in movement of the advice window and display of the route.

Sound effects add considerably to the realism of the student's interaction with the system. These were well-done and effective.

There are many typographic errors in the textual information presented. These are generally trivial and would not cause problems but might occasionally lead to confusion (e.g. "Thick grass gives good concealment; though poor concealment"). Occasionally, feedback fields were empty (examples provided to client). In these cases the message should be adapted to reflect the available information.

User interface in general.

Taking the program as a whole, the user interface is well-designed and attractive. Most features are appropriate to the intended function. Minor problems with specific aspects of the interface are described in the sections above. The presentation would be improved with more video views and more sound effects to enhance realism and involvement. Better colour design would improve the graphical simulation views. The number of buttons used should be minimized; for example, in the tutorial, and the 'continue' function could be removed. In general, the initiative in terms of carrying out actions should be left with the user.

7.3.4.2 Expert Evaluation Summary

Quality of Instruction Methods and Guidance

```
Very                                              Very
Poor          Poor        Average        Good     Good
|______________|______________|______X___|______________|
```

Weaknesses with the advice from the tutor need to be improved to avoid confusion. The simpler forms of guidance work best. The overall logic of the training approach is good, but the initiative for action should be left with the student. The animation sequences, however, could unfold without use of the 'continue' button. This would improve the pace of the interaction. The approach to instruction succeeds in involving the students in the topic.

Quality of Design

```
Very                                              Very
Poor          Poor        Average        Good     Good
|______________|______________|______________X___________|
```

The design is in general well conceived and executed. The video and graphic views, and sound effects make the package engaging and fun to use. Overall layout and design of screens and buttons is good. There are quite a large number of minor typographic errors in the textual material presented.

Quality of Program

```
    Very                                              Very
    Poor          Poor         Average      Good      Good
    |______________|______________|__________|___X_______|
```

The program has very few significant bugs and takes account of the potential variety of student responses well.

Quality of Training Content

```
    Very                                              Very
    Poor          Poor         Average      Good      Good
    |______________|______________|______X___|___________|
```

The training content of the main program is adequate. The main training problem is to get across the skills of operational planning in the context of particular situations. Success with this would be improved with more missions and situations. The relatively more straightforward task of learning the sequence of events leading up to the planning stage is well catered for. The tutorial provides all the reference material needed to succeed with the main program. The main program should provide a broader range of situations to practice skills. The package seems to work well in combination with other forms of training.

7.3.5 Summary of Findings and Design Recommendations

The most important results are those that reveal changes in students' performance as a result of using the training software. The findings from the first trial are very clear-cut: the software was clearly effective in improving student performance, as revealed by the much better scores by the post-CAI group than by the pre-CAI and the control groups.

In the second trial, the performance improvement through the use of the software was less impressive but was still significant. The post-CAI scores were the highest of the four groups and were significantly better than all the groups who had not experienced the software, except the post-control group.

The fact that the software yielded a less dramatic improvement in the second trial than in the first may be due to the fact that there was a longer delay between the pre- and post-conditions, during which the students undertook their normal training. In the first trial, all testing took place after students had completed their normal training. The most effective use of the software might thus be as an after-training 'booster'. The improvement from using the software in this way was quite dramatic. We can conclude that the software is effective in consolidating and adding value to the existing military training programme.

The attitude assessments revealed that, on the whole, the software was popular with students and does not suffer from any major usability problems. Students found the program interesting, well-organized, and easy to understand. They also felt that it was an appropriate way of learning military strategy and tactics. Instructors, who might be expected to be more critical than their students, also reacted favourably to most aspects of the program. Comments from a few users suggested that realism could be improved, particularly in terms of graphics and the number and variety of missions. Most indicated that they would like to spend more time using systems such as this.

Expert assessment of the package was generally favourable. Minor bugs and typographic mistakes in the tutorial module should be easily corrected. The provision of help should be reconsidered. Currently, users almost never explicitly request help, including use of the tutorial, through the pull-down Help menu. It may be better to remove this option and rely on the tutoring component to detect when guidance is needed. The tutorial might be better regarded as a separate training program to be used alone or before a session on the system. In this case, there should be explicit testing of users' knowledge within the tutorial, for each main topic covered. Users would have to succeed on a particular topic before they could move on to another.

Although the interaction between the user and system is generally robust, in the sense that the student would generally not be seriously misled or be forced to abandon the training, the tutoring component does need some refinement. Currently, students are likely to encounter contradictory or circular advice during the choice of the sequence of activities. At the planning stage the advice does not always accurately reflect the most recently made plan. This is likely to cause considerable confusion and should be corrected. It is better to be less ambitious but accurate in the advice given than attempting to provide very sophisticated advice that may not match the users' perceptions exactly. The strategy of carrying the action forward by having the tutor make decisions for the student is probably ill-advised. Usually the student was notified of the action taken but this is not very salient during a planning session. Sometimes it appeared that action was taken without the student being informed. Confusion often arose from the use of the 'Continue' key; it is not always clear what is continuing and sometimes the advice associated with these situations did not seem to make sense. It would be better to simply let the animation play through its moves, allowing the student to interrupt if he wished. Visually, the animation works well.

Video views of locations are not of sufficient resolution or continuity to fulfill their function of giving a good all round impression of the terrain. A continuous 360 degree view or motion sequence should be used. If a large amount of video material is to be incorporated in training systems in the future, the use of an analogue-storage videodisk should be considered. The sound effects used are very effective and enhance the realism of the training enormously. A few more examples could be included to add to student involvement with the situation. Videodisks also provide a relatively efficient way of storing larger amounts of sound.

The numerous, minor typographic errors contained in the textual information presented to students should be corrected. Students should not have to move text windows; it would be better have a clearly marked button for closing the window.

7.3.6 Summary Recommendations

- Have a separate tutorial program incorporating evaluation (could be used before and after to evaluate the software).

- Keep tutoring simple, concentrating on accuracy of advice in relation to students' current situation and most recent events.

- Although advice is essential, action initiative should remain with the student.

- Use interactive videodisk technology to facilitate the incorporation of larger amounts of higher resolution video views of locations.

- Use more sound effects to improve fidelity and student involvement.

- Increase the number of missions and variety of situations.

- It is likely that the program is best used after conventional training, although the effects of varying the timing should be investigated.

- In future CAI applications of this type, more value will be added by increasing the multimedia aspects of the presentation, improving realism and involvement, than in attempting to make the tutor more sophisticated ("intelligent").

7.4   COMPARISON OF MANUAL AND AUTOMATIC HYPERMEDIA LINKING

7.4.1   Introduction

Studies of hypermedia usability have typically focused on aspects such as comprehension of materials, recall of facts, and speed or success in information retrieval tasks. This was the approach used in the experiment reported in Chapter 6. And as we saw in Chapter 4, comparisons have often been made between hypermedia presentations and traditional linear arrangement of materials, with hypermedia typically faring the less well. Such tests of overall usability are analogous to the assessment described in sections 7.2 and 7.3.

In this section, I describe a study to assess one component of a hypermedia system; the quality of links between text nodes. The study was motivated by a project to develop successful means of automatically generating such links (HEFTI - Hypertext Extraction From Text Incrementally - see Chignell *et al.*, in press), and the need to compare such linking with that of a human author. It provides an example of analytical assessment of a particular system feature, as opposed to the global evaluation of a complete application described earlier in the chapter. Often, such analytic evaluation will be prior to a full-blown assessment; this is usually a natural part of the development path for a well-designed multimedia application.

Browsing through a typical hypermedia system involves viewing a node, selecting a link (that is, choosing another node to move to next) and then viewing the chosen next node. This process is then repeated until browsing is finished (see Figure 7.1).

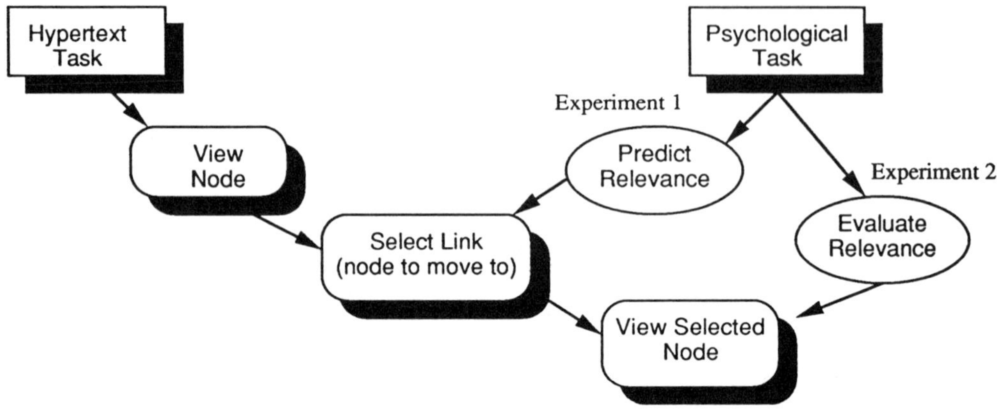

Figure 7.1 - Psychological tasks and hypertext tasks

Evaluating the quality of the links was the main focus of the study. Judgements of quality (by hypermedia users) may be made before they are traversed (from the descriptor provided to permit selection) or after they have been traversed (from viewing the target node in the light of the user's interests). The first has been termed predicted relevance, and the latter evaluated relevance (see Nordhausen *et al.*, 1991).

The first experiment to be described assessed evaluated relevance; the second looked at predicted relevance. In both experiments we compared automatically generated links with manually authored ones. We also included links generated between nodes by random assignment, to provide a control condition against which both the other methods of link generation could be compared. We expected both to be superior to random linking. For a method of automatic linking to be acceptable, we would expect it to be rated as highly as manual linking, or nearly so. It might even be the case that automatic linking could be judged as superior, since human authors find the process of linking laborious and may not be particularly thorough or consistent in their assignment of links between nodes.

7.4.2 Experiment One: Assessing Evaluated Relevance of Links

7.4.2.1 Method

A hypertext system was developed such that subjects were asked to rate the degree of relationship between two nodes just after they had traversed the link from one to the other. Figure 7.2 shows a screen from this system where a node on a particular topic is being viewed. On the right of the screen is the similarity rating scale with the finger pointing roughly midway along the scale. Users of this modified system must indicate their rating of the degree of similarity between the two nodes on the scale before they can continue browsing. The position of the pointer is then used to derive a similarity value of between 0 (very dissimilar) and 100 (very similar).

Twenty students from a knowledge engineering course at ISS served as subjects in the experiment. They had little or no experience in using a hypertext system. The material for the hypertext document was taken from a text on artificial intelligence and was highly relevant to the course for which the students were registered. In total, the material consisted of about 10,000 words on expert systems, and was converted into a hypertext document of 29 text nodes. Reference links led to pop-up nodes containing figures and tables, but our interest was in the related links that provided the facility for browsing around the 29 text nodes. Subjects were randomly assigned to three experimental groups with each group experiencing a differently linked version of the document, although the reference links, the nodes and the text and other material they contained were identical. One group experienced the manually authored links, another the HEFTI-generated links, and the third the randomly linked version. All three versions had, on average, the same number of links available from each node. The author of the handcrafted version was, in fact, the author of the textbook from which the material was extracted (Patterson, 1990).

Subjects in each of the three experimental groups were asked to browse the material in the hypertext system for a total of 20 minutes. As they did so, their similarity ratings for each link traversed was collected by the system and logged in a file for later analysis. They were then given a comprehension test of ten multiple choice questions, which was meant to assess their assimilation of the material they had browsed.

We also administered a subjective attitude questionnaire covering aspects such as ease of use, sufficiency of number of choices available, and general impressions of the system, using a 7-point scale where 1 corresponded to a very low rating and 7 to a very high rating.

7.4.2.2   Results

Table 7.1 shows the mean values for each of the dependent variables used, and for each of the three methods of creating links. The similarity scores were taken from the 100-point scale ratings, and the comprehension scores were obtained by adding up the number of correct answers for the ten multiple choice questions, whereas the others came from the 7-point scale ratings.

Measure	Manual	Automatic	Random
Similarity	36.0	54.4	44.3
Comprehension	6.9	7.0	5.5
Enough links?	2.6	2.7	3.0
Useful choices?	2.9	3.7	3.7*
Ease of use?	3.4	4.6	4.3**

$(*p< .05, **p< .01)$

Table 7.1 - Mean results across the three types of link

Rather surprisingly, the highest similarity score was obtained for the version with automatically generated links, and the lowest for the manual version. But an analysis of variance revealed that these differences were not statistically significant. In other words, in terms of rated similarity of links, the three treatments had not affected subjects' ratings of the degree of similarity of pairs of nodes. There was, however, a highly significant difference between ease of use for the three methods of linking $(F[2,17]=6.50, p< .005)$, with automatically-generated links rated more usable than the manually-created ones. This finding was supported by a significant difference between the three methods in terms of the rated usefulness of choices offered $(F[2,17]=3.64, p< .05)$. Again, the same trend was observed, with manual linking coming out worse than automatic linking.

We were interested in knowing the nature of the difference in ease of use between the three linking methods. Post-hoc statistical tests, to compare ease of use between the three methods, revealed that manual linking was significantly worse than both random and automatic linking ($p <$ .05 and $p <$ .01, respectively), but that automatic and random linking were not different from each other in terms of rated ease of use. One of the joys (and torments) of carrying out experimental tests of ideas is that the findings are very often so surprising that a major rethink is required.

7.4.3   Experiment Two: Assessing Predicted Relevance of Links

7.4.3.1 Method

To assess the predicted relevance of links generated by the three methods already described, we constructed a protean document by converting a large portion of a textbook on local area network technology. We finished up with a hypermedia document of about 30,000 words segmented into 111 nodes. This was then converted into linked hypermedia by applying automatic linking, random linking, and hand-crafted linking as in the first experiment. The human author was an expert in the topic area and was very familiar with the textbook in question. Unlike the previous case, however, we did not create three different versions corresponding to the three treatments. Rather, we took equal numbers of each link type and mixed them within one hypermedia version. We did this by randomly choosing 83 links from each set, making a set of 246 bi-directional links in all. There was a small amount of overlap between links created by the three different methods of generation, and we arrived at a distribution of 85 manual links, 89 automatic links, and 93 random links.

Forty-nine students from a Systems Analysis class at ISS participated in the experiment. Each one experienced the same hypermedia version containing all three types of link. They were instructed to browse through the material with the goal of learning about the topic of multi-layered networks, and were told that they would be assessed on this afterwards. Each subject had a period of two hours to browse through the hypermedia.

Our main dependent measure was the number of links chosen of each type. Choosing a link was taken to mean that subjects predicted (from its title) that it would be relevant. Since the three types were mixed, we could compare the number of links of each type chosen as a measure of the predicted relevance of a linking method. Figure 7.2 shows the screen display when a user is ready to move on from the node she has been reading by selecting one of the offered links. Every link selection made is thus a forced choice between the different types of link. Subjects' choices were stored in a transaction log for later analysis. The subjects themselves were not aware of this logging, nor were they informed about the three different link types.

7.4.3.2 Results

We performed a 1-way analysis of variance on the frequency of usage of the three types of link. This was significant ($F[2,96]=31.2$, $p< .001$), and post-hoc comparisons showed that that this was due to significantly more manually created links being selected than either of the other two types (50.1 selections per subject, versus 33.5 for random and 28.4 for automatically generated links). The difference between random and automatic was not significant. We also calculated the degree of correlation between frequencies of use of each link type and scores on the comprehension test. We found no correlation between comprehension test performance and the type of link a subject tended to choose.

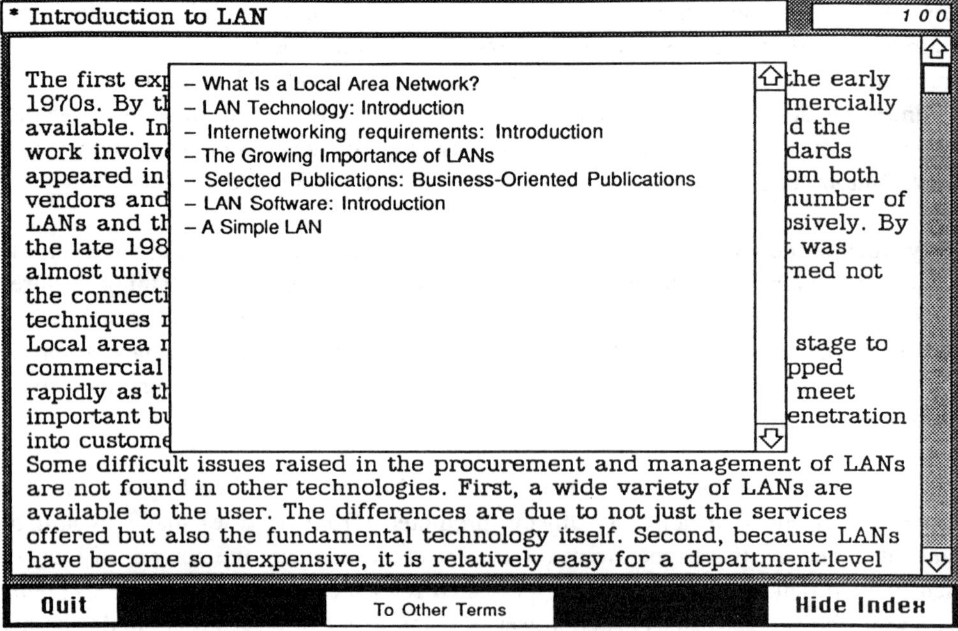

Figure 7.2 - Selecting a link in Experiment 2

7.4.4 Discussion

The results from our two experiments are remarkably incompatible. In the first one, we were surprised to find that automatic links were no better than random ones, but even more surprised that manual links came out worst of all. How could random links be better than those created by the human author? In the second experiment manual links were clearly preferred to the other two types, but we again found no difference between random and automatic. So taking the two experiments together we would be forced to conclude that our method of automatically linking hypermedia nodes is no better than linking them at random.

One way of accounting for the different results from the two experiments is to point to the different assessment methods used. Several subjects complained that the method of evaluating relevance, by completing a link relevance rating after every selection, was very tedious and intruded into the browsing task. But there seems no obvious way that this would impact differently on ratings of different types of link. So we cannot account for manual links faring so badly in the first experiment, but well in the second. That comprehension scores were not correlated with choice of link type suggests that comprehension is little affected by the types of link used, although another possibility is simply that our comprehension test was too crude a measure for this evaluation. Taken together, however, we would be forced to conclude from both sets of results that we may as well use random linking, since this is rapidly and easily achieved.

This perhaps tells us most about the nature of browsing in hypermedia, at least with the kind of material used here. It seems that with a relatively small amount of material from a single source, subjects can make sense of a link between virtually any two nodes. It may be that a large hypermedia system on diverse topics would reveal different effects, but here again we may simply be indulging in wishfully thinking that hypermedia, based around the notion of following links to explore connections between nuggets of information, *must* be good for *something*.

APPENDIX 1

STUDENT ATTITUDE QUESTIONNAIRE

In this quick test, we are trying to find out what you (the student) think about the training system you have been using.

Instructions

Please answer the questions by putting a cross on the scale, to show what you think..
For example, if the question asked :

"How often would you like to use systems like this?"

You would mark a point on the scale to show how you felt, e.g.

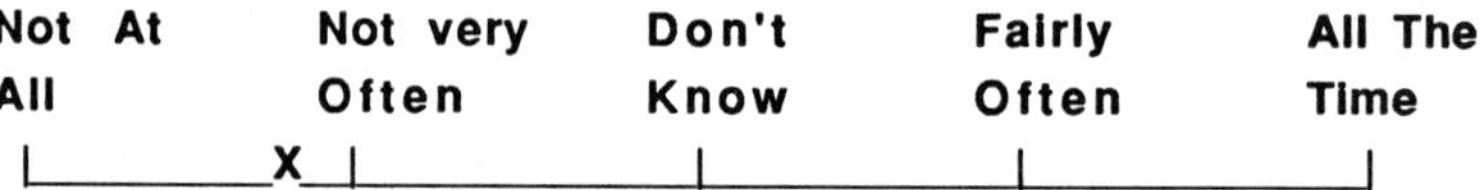

The cross shows that you don't want to use systems like this very often.

Now answer the following questions by marking the scale to show how **you** feel about the training system you have just used.

Remember, we are testing the system, not you.

Try and avoid picking the middle ('Don't Know') part of the scale.

Please answer quickly without spending too long on each question.

Answer all the questions.

Student's Name: Results averaged from all students in first trial.

First Trial (Students)

[Overall Mean Rating] - 3.7 (out of 5)

[Personal Affect] - 3.8

1 How interesting did you find using the system?

```
Very            Quite           Don't Know    A Bit         Very
Interesting     Interesting                   Boring        Boring
|______X___|________________|______________|_____________|______________|
```

2 How varied?

```
Very            A Bit           Don't Know    Quite         Very
Monotonous      Monotonous                    Varied        Varied
|_______________|_______________|______X______|_____________|______________|
```

3 Were you active or passive in using the system?

```
Very            Quite           Neither       Quite         Very
Active          Active                         Passive       Passive
|______________|_X______________|_____________|_____________|______________|
```

4 Are you happy with your performance?

```
Very            Unhappy         Don't Know    Happy         Very
Unhappy                                                      Happy
|_______________|_______________|_X___________|_____________|______________|
```

5 Would you like to use the system again?

Definitely   Yes   Don't Know   No   Definitely
Yes   Not

L_______X__|____________|____________|____________|

6 Were you glad when the training session was over?

Definitely   Yes   Don't Know   No   Definitely
Yes   Not

L___________|____________|____X____|____________|

7 Do you think systems like this should be used more in military training?

Definitely   Yes   Don't Know   No   Definitely
Yes   Not

L_______X__|____________|____________|____________|

[Systematic Arrangement] - 3.9

8 How well organized was the training?

Chaotic   Dis-   Don't Know   Quite   Very Well
                  organized   Good   Organized

L___________|____________|____X_|____________|

9 Did the training seem to occur in the right order, or was it mixed up?

Very Well   Quite   Don't Know   Poorly   Completely
Ordered   Good   Ordered   Mixed Up

L_______X__________|____________|____________|

[Task Relevance] - 3.9

10 Did you get a lot of information from using the system?

Very Little	Not Much	Don't Know	Quite A Lot	Very Much Information

11 Will the training help you in the field?

Definitely Yes	Probably	Don't Know	Probably Not	Definitely Not

[Understandability] - 3.8

12 How clear were the instructions about how to use the system?

Very Clear	Quite Clear	Don't Know	Not Clear	Very Unclear

13 How easy to understand was the system as a whole?

Very Difficult	Quite Difficult	Don't Know	Quite Easy	Very Easy

14 How easy was the written information to follow?

Very Easy	Quite Easy	Don't Know	Quite Difficult	Very Difficult

[Components] - 3.0

15 How often did you refer to the information in the tutorial component?

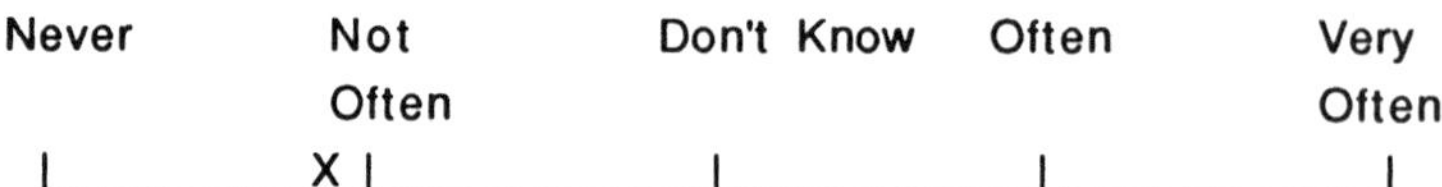

Never	Not Often	Don't Know	Often	Very Often

16 How realistic were the situations you came across?

Very Realistic	Quite Realistic	Don't Know	Quite Unrealistic	Very Unrealistic

17 Did you feel in control of what happened?

Not At All	Not Much	Don't Know	Most Of The Time	All The Time

18 How useful was the advice you were given?

Very Useful	Quite Useful	Don't Know	Not Much Use	Useless

[Credibility] - 3.9

19 Do you think the information in the system is correct?

Not Usually	Not Always	Don't Know	Usually	Yes, Always

20 Could you rely on what you learned from the system, when you are in the field?

```
Yes,            Sometimes    Don't Know    Not          No,
Always                                     Much         Never
|________X___________|____________|____________|
```

[Suitability] - 3.7

21 Was this training relevant to you?

```
Not             Not          Don't Know    Quite        Yes,
At All          Very                       Relevant     Very

|____________|____________|___X____|____________|
```

22 Is this method of training appropriate?

```
Very            Quite        Don't Know    Not Very     Not At All
Appropriate     Appropriate                Appropriate  Appropriate
|__________|_X______|____________|____________|
```

23 How complete is the training? In other words, did the training cover everything you need to know about this topic?

```
Very            Incomplete    Don't Know    Quite        Complete
Sketchy                                     Complete
|____________|____________|___X___|____________|
```

[Workload] - 3.7

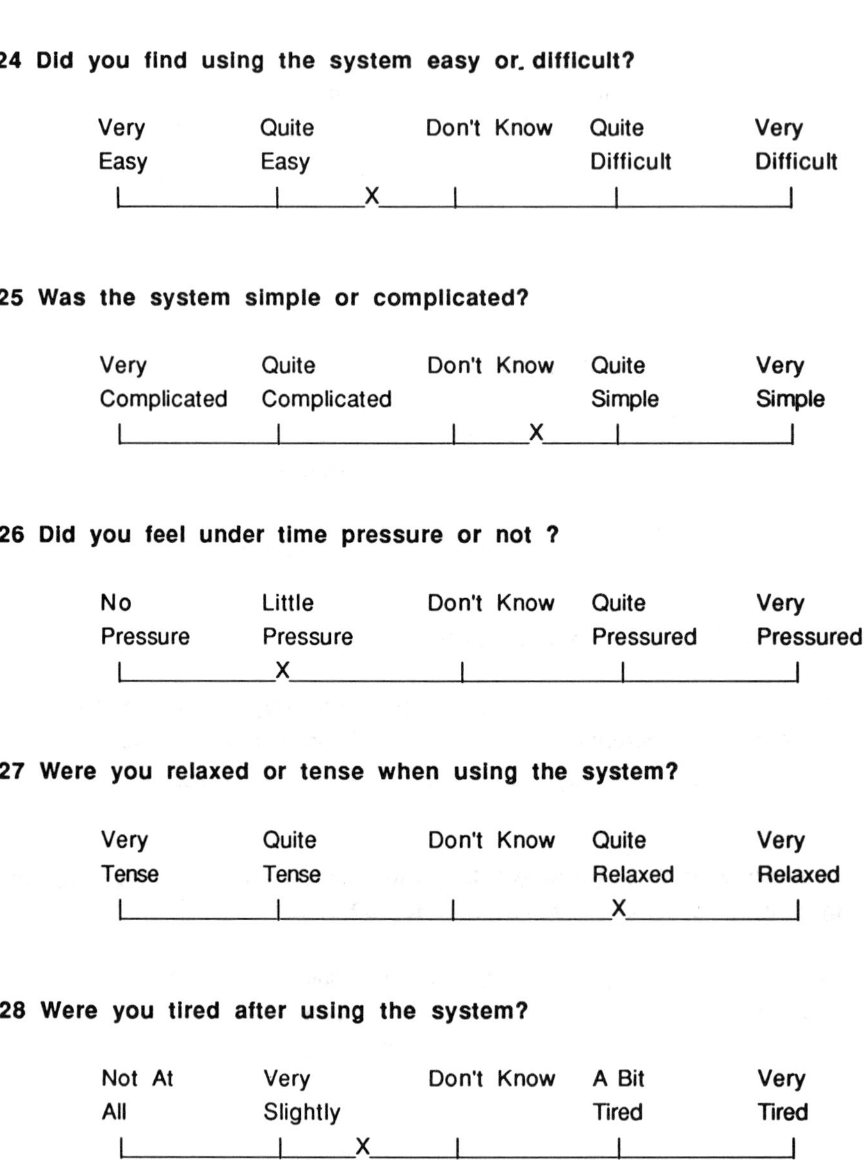

24 Did you find using the system easy or. difficult?

25 Was the system simple or complicated?

26 Did you feel under time pressure or not ?

27 Were you relaxed or tense when using the system?

28 Were you tired after using the system?

Any other comments you would like to make about the training system?

Thank you for your cooperation.

Chapter 8

Desirable Futures?

"Humankind cannot stand very much reality"

- T S Eliot, *Burnt Norton*

"Humankind ....cannot stand too little reality"

- Pico Iyer, *Video Night in Kathmandu*

The success of information systems already depends to a significant extent on the suitability and appeal of the way users interact with those systems. This trend will be strengthened as multimedia applications proliferate over the next few years. With interaction based on hypermedia and virtual world models, the interface of user and system penetrates deep into the information base itself. This is in sharp contrast to earlier systems, where the user has a narrow window on what is available, and is once removed from directly accessing contents and functionalities.

Users will increasingly interact with artificial realities, representing informational worlds with natural and supernatural characteristics. This will entail major changes in art, entertainment, communication, and society in general. As with all dramatic new developments, not all the consequences will be benign. For some practical purposes, there will be integration of direct manipulation and conversational methods of interaction. A navigation-based approach will be supplemented with more traditional, computer-mediated search facilities. These may often take the form of computer "agents" that are given a query to deal with and report their findings back to the user at his convenience.

Interface design will be guided by the quest for 'natural' ways of interaction and users' task demands, though these will often be in conflict. Interfaces will increasingly be built up from kits by users. The kits will themselves become more complex and specialized

The virtual world approach is heavily dependent on hardware. New devices for stereoscopic, 3-D vision, tactile feedback, three-dimensional sound, and new input methods for harnessing motor responses are needed. These are already appearing, but are currently either expensive, crude and uncomfortable, or both. Ideally, such devices will become unobtrusive. In the long run, they may even be surgically implanted. In the longer term, genetic engineering is a possibility. In advanced countries, people will spend increasing amounts of time in virtual worlds.

8.1 THE IT REVOLUTION: HERESIES AND DOGMAS

8.1.1 Introduction

There is no doubt that the development of interactive multimedia systems will dramatically accelerate the rate at which computer technology penetrates into the everyday life and work of the majority of people. Not only will the level of penetration be increased, the nature of the relationship between people and technology will be fundamentally and irreversibly changed.

We are already beginning to see the negative side of an increasing emphasis on "computer literacy" in the home, the school, and the workplace. Brod (1984), in "Technostress" chronicles the detrimental effects on the quality of life, interpersonal relationships, and mental health, of holding computational machinery, and its mastery, as the ultimate model of ideal human fulfillment. He argues that in the process of adopting and adapting to increasingly ubiquitous computer technology, we are in danger of losing sight of our true selves, our human nature. The claim is that the currently neglected human element underlies our most meaningful and significant accomplishments: in science, the arts, and physical endeavour. Information technology is seductive, and mankind has a tendency to model itself on whatever is the current source of mass seduction, be this religion, capitalism, natural science, Hollywood romance, or the data processing view of intelligent behaviour fostered by computer scientists.

On the other hand, Shotton (1989) paints a picture of computer absorption as a benign phenomenon. She suggests that for people who are naturally more comfortable with non-social activities than with other people, computer technology provides solace, stimulation, excitement and even inspiration. Why would anyone want to deny these rather lonely people such harmless pleasure? And yet, the way computing systems are developing, the very characteristics that these reclusive types enjoy about them - their complexity, predictability, and fundamental seriousness (as opposed to the frivolity of mankind) - are being replaced by a richness of experience and personal engagement that they may find threatening.

8.1.2   Heresies and Dogmas of the Information Age

It is not contentious to assume that the current blossoming of computer-based applications in various settings is changing the quality of work, leisure, and creative activity for large numbers of people. How that change will be affected by the move towards multimedia interaction with computers is the main focus of the current chapter. First of all, let us consider a few heresies and dogmas of the "Information Revolution", which is the starting point for these developments.

8.1.2.1 Heresies

1. Computers are not intrinsically important.

2. Anything that matters can be done without computers.

3. The IT "revolution" has no purpose. That is why we are desperately trying to find things to do with the technology, rather than vice versa.

4. Computer solutions are generally not cost effective. IT does not make economic sense, except to computer manufacturers.

5. IT is reducing our leisure time, our autonomy, our creativity, and our quality of life.

6. Rather than computers becoming more human-like, humanity is becoming more machine-like.

These heresies represent things that almost cannot be said in educated discourse today. That is unfortunate, but tells us something about the power of technology politics. That power is not so much a reflection of what has been created by technological means as a system of values, a vision of man and his world, that is now very pervasive indeed. We are putting our faith in computer technology, having lost faith in religions, politics, and society.

8.1.2.2 Dogmas

1. Multimedia systems can become "playgrounds of the mind".

2. Multimedia is better than text.

3. Multimedia is for everyone.

The new faith demands the acceptance of certain dogmas. Although we have not developed the machines that make these views irresistible, the promise is there and is embraced by large numbers of people. Actually, there is nothing that has yet been created that would qualify as a playground of the mind. We are beginning to create computer-based playgrounds, using different media, incorporating interactivity, and that are claimed to be as involving and entertaining as their physical counterparts and are promised to become more so. But there is no evidence that this is a positive step in terms of education, mental health, or quality of life.

Part of the claim for the benefits of multimedia interaction is that it allows people to think in new ways, to develop better understanding, to gain insights that are not possible if one is confined to text. This seems to confuse the internal experience of exercising the intellect with the media we use for communicating our ideas. Krueger (1991) makes the point forcefully when he comments that his vision of the future of multimedia systems "reintegrates the mind and the body, which have been estranged since the printing press created the sensory-deprivation, black-and-white world of the intellect, and offers a knowledge environment in which the mind, the body, and the full sensorium are employed" (p261).

Of course, there certainly are times when text is not the best means to communicate ideas, even to ourselves. Scientific visualization of complex physical, chemical and biological phenomena is an obvious example. It could even be claimed that what we know as education deliberately discriminates in favour of those who are more comfortable with the abstract symbols of language than with manipulating the varied and messy objects that comprise the physical world. Multimedia technology can thus be seen as reversing this centuries-old tendency.

The other dogma is that multimedia is somehow for everyone, whereas existing sources of knowledge are for the privileged few. Krueger again makes the point clearly when he suggests that "the concept touches every aspect of life, it is an intellectual feast to which everyone is invited" (p261). But books are cheaper than computers, and when our party requires all guests to have access to advanced computing systems, we are really talking about the better off people in the richer countries of the world, and it is difficult to see that basic economic fact changing in the near future.

Even if the claims seem overstated, there is no doubt that a revolution of sorts is underway. Interactive multimedia is a truly new phenomenon that will change the lives and outlooks of large numbers of people. To make that point a little more clearly, in the next section I outline a vision of what is possible in the future by means of a hypothetical model of multimedia interaction. I then discuss in a little more detail the nature and possible effects of the pervasive adoption of "artificial realities" (also known by the less self-contradictory title of "virtual worlds") which comprise the leading edge of work on multimedia.

8.2   VISIONS OF A VIRTUAL FUTURE

8.2.1   Information City

Imagine a system based around the overarching metaphor of a holiday visit to Information City. Elements of the metaphor include:

A hostess - who welcomes you to the resort, and finds out whether this is your first visit, and if not, accesses the records of your previous trips. She informs you about some of the facilities on offer, finds out about your interests and aims, and suggests a good way to start your holiday.

This is done principally in conversation, using demonstrations of the resort's many attractions and facilities, videos of other happy holiday-makers enjoying themselves, and so on.

She also reminds you that the proprietors are always happy to receive new information from visitors. You are glad you remembered to pack your CD.

Before leaving the reception area, the hostess encourages you to sign up for one or two tours, suggesting a couple that might set you off in the direction you want to travel.

She also shows you how to explore under your own steam, either by leaving directly from reception, or by taking a tour part way, then hopping off in the area you want to explore.

Amongst the many facilities you learn to use, both from the hostess, and during the course of you stay at the resort, are the following:

Organized tours of famous landmarks.

During the time the resort has been open for business, many popular tourist trails have been established. A good initial way to find out about your area of interest is to take one of these, benefiting from the experience of previous travellers and the information presented to you by the guide who accompanies every tour.

Unlike some commercial tours, which offer no escape for the punter who gets bored, you are free to leap off the bus at any convenient point. The chances of this are minimized by the fact that the hostess has tried to protect you from being pestered by tour operators who offer trips you are unlikely to find relevant or interesting.

But as you familiarize yourself with the lie of the land, the time will come when you want to be more adventurous, and explore on your own.

The landscape of Information City has been specially designed to meet the needs of wandering knowledge seekers. In fact, the features of the landscape actually change over time as a function of just how interesting such holidaymakers find them.

Navigating around the city reveals an unfolding 3-D landscape of colourful structures, coming in all shapes and sizes. Exploration is effortless as you are free to drift between, within, or above the buildings at any speed you choose.

If you lose your bearings, you can fly high above the city, descending towards a familiar landmark to re-orient yourself, before dropping down towards an area of particular interest. The hostess also gave you a map of the city, highlighting those areas that she thought would be of interest to you.

The layout of the city is memorable, although it is not static; fortunately, facilities seem to be very conveniently arranged. In general, the colour and shape of a structure are useful for memorising where you have been. Similarly coloured buildings tend to have related contents; they also tend to be grouped together in 'villages'.

The size of a building generally indicates its importance. Importance is determined partly by the sheer volume of its contents, but also by the number of times it has been visited, and the number of different places it has been visited from. Buildings that have not been visited recently tend to gradually shrink and migrate towards the outskirts of their village.

Certain distinctive structures serve as landmarks, but do not store information except about other buildings. They can point you in the right direction when you lose your bearings. If required, they can set up 'magic corridors' which will take you instantly to any point in the city

One very helpful feature of all buildings is the information booth in the foyer. Apart from the directory and floorplan, this is usually staffed by experts on the type of information available within the building. They are happy to process your queries on any topic within their area, or can contact an expert in related fields.

Further inside the buildings, you can select information in almost any form, with animation, 3-D, stereo sound, and all the facilities you would expect of a high-tech, evolving knowledge-based resort. In some areas, crowds of authors obscure your view of parts of the information. In others, you yourself contribute a few items. And, of course, every step you take, and every item you examine or add, makes a small change to the shape of the city.

After your stay at Information City, you return home tired but somehow invigorated, having found lots of the kind of information you were after, and added a few ideas of your own. You are also happy in the knowledge that the City is now a different place because of your visit, and that every time you visit it again, you can look at it afresh.

8.2.2   An Institutional Example

Developing on this model of a virtual informational world, the following presents a slightly more focused look, taking the Institute of Systems Science as an element of the City (the 'Intelligent Island' and city-state of Singapore).

The building has a distinctive shape and style, and is easily spotted on the map (if you are navigating at street level) or from your 'copter (if you are taking a structural overview of the City), and of course it features on most of the guided tours of computer science information, a major concentration of buildings within the gigantic Science Park. It is somewhat removed from its neighbours, to emphasize the special topics it covers. This tends to reduce the number of 'visitors' who stumble upon it during unfocused topic browsing.

The layout of the building, as is usual in Info City, reflects the information that can be accessed within it. In the entrance/exit area there are floor plans of all levels, and a display illustrating how this building relates to others you may have come from, or choose to go to next. Selecting the forth floor will take you straight to the Director. You can either consult him directly on the work of ISS in a question-and-answer session, or watch his pre-recorded introductory video featuring examples of the work in progress, history, and so on. The Director is always available, but you will probably decide to explore the building yourself, perhaps going back later to ask a few more questions.

From the third floor plan you can choose from several labs in which a variety of projects are being demonstrated: information systems, multi-lingual interaction, neural nets, multimedia database research, hypermedia, and so on. You are able to try out many of the systems yourself, as they are fully integrated within the building, and the City. You become a little disorientated when you find that Information City IS one of these systems. Topic experts are also on hand for detailed consultation of the technical issues.

The second floor library is one of the most advanced of its kind, holding its entire stock of books and journals on optical disks. Almost any text on systems science and related topics can be accessed from here. Because of the rich indexing of terms, cross-linked in hypertext fashion, natural language search and browsing can be combined to locate a particular article, or survey a general topic area, to meet the needs of the user. In fact, indexing occupies more storage space than the texts themselves.

Also on the second floor, the teaching facility offers a range of multimedia lectures, tutorials, and practical sessions, pitched at various levels to suit the needs of the learner. Computer-aided learning techniques, based on highly interactive sessions on selected topic areas, and tracking and adapting to the learner's progress, are popular with the more serious students. You are free to take as much, or little tuition as you choose; personal progress profiles are maintained to provide a continuing, individualized teaching programme over separate learning sessions.

By this time you have learned a lot, and are ready for some light relief. You decide to take a 'copter from the entrance and soar above the city, dropping down into the unmistakable luridly coloured heart of Sci-fi Village. What you want now is to explore new worlds, and battle it out with a few thousand aliens, via the Interplanetary Gateway. Culture can wait till tomorrow.

8.2.3   Comments

The scenarios above are caricatures of course, but are technically feasible in the not-too-long term. In the first one, the spatial metaphor is quite well maintained, although the concept of topic experts was introduced to assist with the location of specific items of information. In the second example, this tendency is emphasized more strongly as the application needs are more task-related. This seems to be a general characteristic of multimedia. A purely physical metaphor, based on user-controlled exploration of three-dimensional space is very appealing, but may be more appropriate for entertainment than for practical tasks involving locating particular items of information. Virtual realities encourage a style of exploration that is analogous to the physical exploration of 3-D space. This is likely to be very engaging, but will need to be enhanced with other functionalities to be of practical use.

8.3   VIRTUAL WORLDS: THE BEST AND THE WORST OF EVERYTHING

Whatever the shortcomings of the purely physical metaphor suggested by the creation of virtual worlds, there seems little doubt that future multimedia systems will continue the current trend in that direction, though enhanced with additional non-physical features. Given the momentum that these developments are building up, we are likely to see virtual worlds portrayed as the answer to all issues in multimedia interaction, carried forward, often unconsciously, by the unquestioned dogmas of the information age. In the longer term, a more thoughtful approach to harnessing the great potential of multimedia might emerge, though the marketplace is likely to determine developments rather than any scientific agenda. Some applications will thrive, others will wither. Multimedia may be the next big thing in entertainment and mass communication, after television, karaoke and rented videos. It may become a forum for personal communication, supplementing or replacing the telephone, E-mail, talk-lines, and bulletin boards. It may become the primary medium of artistic expression. It will have many educational applications, and might even replace education "as we know it". In the rest of this section, we consider some of the positive and negative ramifications of such developments.

8.3.1   The Redundancy of Literacy

For several years people have speculated about the advent of the paperless office. Increasingly, electronic documents are replacing traditional paper forms. With the advent of multimedia, we are taking this process a quantum leap further; from the paperless information system to the textless. Of course, in the same way that paper has not disappeared from our offices, text will never be completely absent from all information systems. But the importance of text will be reduced, and this will have significant consequences. Our educational systems are currently predominantly text-based. The many years of full-time education most of us experience are in large part devoted to instilling literacy in students. And this does not merely involve acquiring the ability to read and write. Techniques of interpretation and construction, such as how to analyse a complex technical text, or how to put together a convincing argument in a short essay, are the necessary accomplishments of well-educated adults. By the possession of these skills, educated individuals are distinguished from the illiterate masses. But the most convincing multimedia presentation will not necessarily be the one that is best argued, in the sense of a well-constructed and expressed logical statement.

In general, the introduction of multimedia can be seen as a liberalization of the social mechanisms that control access to knowledge and to the opportunity to reach others through "the media". This liberalization is possible because multimedia implies the deskilling of knowledge, the redundancy of techniques of interpretation. With multimedia, the interpretation of information is relatively transparent. In the same way that "computer literacy" is becoming a meaningless term given the increasing transparency of access to computer-based information, so literacy itself may become an outmoded concept. Literacy will give way to "mediacy" - the immediate apprehension of meaning through multimedia interaction. This prospect will fill some individuals with horror, others with a sense of long-awaited freedom. That knowledge should become more widely available should appeal to all but those with a vested interest in social control. The danger is that in the process knowledge will become trivialized, since such strands as the history of ideas will be left out of the fabric of intelligent discourse.

By dividing knowledge into convenient nuggets of information that may be accessed by an infinite variety of routes, we run the risk of decontextualizing what we know. Inappropriate transfer from virtual worlds to the world at large can be characterized as one aspect of such decontextualization of knowledge. But the problem is broader than that. Without appropriate contexts, what passes for knowledge may become literally meaningless. The linearity inherent in history, in constructing an argument, and in the life of an organism may become lost or forgotten.

8.3.2   Everything is Possible, Virtually

I have pointed to a trend, which many see as inevitable, whereby multimedia will be implemented in the form of virtual worlds. Some see these virtual worlds as the ultimate in HCI. But virtual worlds may be a limiting metaphor in some applications, but liberating in others. Certainly, virtual reality is the ultimate WIMP interfaces, where direct manipulation is taken to its extreme. WIMP interfaces (based on the four techniques of windows, icons, menus, and pointing) have been very successful in improving the usability of a wide range of systems. Presenting system entities as objects that can be selected and acted upon at the click of a mouse button has improved the transparency and learnability of many user interfaces. The same is likely to apply to multimedia implemented as virtual reality.

Everyone will be able to move around in multimedia information space and will be able to experience, and put together, collections of multimedia materials for various purposes.

Not everything is best done by direct manipulation, however. It is very suitable for training practical skills, for example, but less so for more abstract topics. Sometimes, its preferable to make a query and have the system attempt to answer it through computer-mediated search. The prediction is that this will be undertaken by computerized "agents" that will be allocated tasks by the user and will report back at times convenient to the user. Not all things are best done by users themselves. Users have little attention to spare on details and will want to delegate much of the legwork, as always. It does not really make any sense to try and locate a particular piece of information by swimming through a sea of multimedia objects, though that would be possible and might throw up some unexpected finds along the way. An interesting question for future research is how roles should be allocated between the human user and computerized agents who will contribute to completing a given user's tasks (see Negroponte, 1989).

Another issue with implementing virtual worlds is the use of physical space as a metaphor for information space. In a virtual world the structure must necessarily be explicit. But how can the semantic dimensions of multimedia information be mapped onto the virtually physical dimensions of our created world? This is the major hurdle that must be overcome if virtual reality is to extend beyond an entertaining way of happening upon distributed fragments of knowledge. It may not be possible to ever use a purely physical metaphor to structure interactions with a semantically rich knowledge base. How can subtle and/or complex abstract ideas be modelled in concrete? We need more research that addresses the issues of multimedia design in the context of users' tasks. Rather than assume that explorable virtual worlds will answer every problem, we should consider what a task-based design might look like, and strive to get a feel for the benefits and limits of particular approaches to interface design.

We should also consider the social impact of widely available virtual words. Most people agree that a major application area for multimedia virtual worlds will be entertainment. Adventure games take on a whole new life when one is immersed in a created world of demons, heroes, princesses and monsters. We will be able to engage in violent combat, cheat, lie, and indulge in simulated sex or sadism without fear of inflicting physical harm on others. No doubt this will be a popular outlet for pent-up frustrations and passions. But Krueger (1991) suggests, "The possibility of inflicting realistic mayhem as Jason in an interactive version of *Friday the 13th* seems dangerous. The unthinkable must become more thinkable if you actually rehearse it, even in a simulated environment".

If moral behaviour is largely a function of social conditioning, what will be the consequence of spending a large amount of time, especially in childhood, in virtual worlds where there is no responsibility since every act can be undone and no-one really gets hurt? The obvious danger is that life becomes seen as less precious because its fragility is forgotten. The virtual world could come to be seen as a metaphor for real life, rather than vice versa. Excessive identification with virtual reality may thus result in "dehumanization" on a scale exceeding that predicted by Brod (1984).

Taken to the extreme, virtual reality has the capability to attract almost religious fervour. Religions are based on the promise of a reality beyond the physical. Virtual worlds seem to deliver the goods. If the semblance is convincing enough, it is not inconceivable such fervour will be carried back from the virtual into the real world, with the disasterous consequences that result when people mistake the imaginary for the real.

8.3.3   More for Everyone (who can afford it)

In may ways, the development of multimedia is a step forward in the democratization of access to knowledge. Some people will be threatened by this; many more will take advantage of the new opportunities. Multimedia tools for students, systems for the home based on snapshots and home videos, integration with real-time telecommunication, will allow ordinary people to access and create interactive multimedia entertainments, archives and educational material, and convey these to others around the developed world. Knowledge will be taken out of the hands of the intelligentsia and made available, actually for the first time, to everyone who lives in a developed country and can afford the initial costs of the equipment. Knowledge will change as a result of this.

As Erickson (1989) comments, "When you change the accessibility of information you may change the way in which it is used. When you change the way it's used, you may change the nature of the information that is recorded. When you change what's recorded, it may no longer be what you wanted to make accessible." In other words, control of access to information will become increasingly difficult for those in authority, perhaps even impossible. We have seen this happen in a small way with electronic mail.

People interact very differently in this medium than with paper mail. Users are generally less polite, spend less time worrying about spelling and grammar, often omitting punctuation, upper-case letters, or even vowels in extreme cases. Although this makes the messages harder to read, this seems relatively unimportant to some users. The new medium produces new priorities; in the case of electronic mail the priority is speed. And because electronic mail can be sent to many users, it can be used as a forum for open debate within an organization, often where such a forum has been completely lacking before. This, naturally makes some managements uncomfortable because they have lost control of what topics can be discussed, when and by whom. The new forum can be used to establish pressure groups and muster support for views which may run against management plans. After an initial period of laissez faire, managements usually impose controls on electronic discussions, although these are hard to police given the volume of messages such systems can generate.

In the same way, multimedia will liberalize the access to information and the communication of ideas within and across organizations. Managements, and in some societies governments, will try to control this process. Such attempts seem unlikely to succeed in the long term since they run against an irresistible technological trend.

Finally, it is worth reiterating the view that hypertext and multimedia really are epoch-making developments resulting from storage and communication of information in accessible, electronic form. They give us the potential, if we are clever enough, to build the ultimate responsive information artefacts. And this is a process in which everyone (with the necessary resources) can join. Issues such as the organization of information, navigation, disorientation, browser design and other such things are serious challenges, but are really only red herrings that distract attention from the fact that multimedia is a vast new canvas for self-expression and communication, for better or worse. Seen in this light, current developments are as important, and as irreversible, as the invention of papyrus and, later, the printing press. The opportunities are at least as great as the dangers.

Bibliography

Adar, R. (1989) - "Integrated Interfaces Based on a Theory of Context and Goal Tracking". In Bouwhis, D. G., Taylor, M. M. and Neel, F. (eds.) - The Structure of Multimodal Dialogues. Amsterdam: North Holland.

Akscyn, R., Yoder, E. and McCracken, D. (1988) - "The Data Model is the Heart of Interface Design". In Proceedings of CHI'88, Conference on Human Factors in Computing Systems. New York: ACM.

Alty, J.L. (1991) - "Multimedia - What is It and How do we Exploit It?". In People and Computer VI, Diaper, D. and Hammond N. (eds), Cambridge University Press.

Alty, J.L., Mullin, J. and Weir, G. (1986) - "Survey of Dialogue Systems and Literature on Dialogue Design". Scottish HCI Centre Report No AMU8701/01S, University of Strathclyde, Glasgow.

Apple Computer Inc (1987) - Human Interface Guidelines. Reading, Mass, USA: Addison-Wesley.

Bailey, R.W. (1982) - Human Performance Engineering: a guide for system designers. Englewood Cliffs, NJ: Prentice-Hall.

Baird, P. and Percival, M. (1989) - "Glasgow Online: database development using Apple's HyperCard". In Hypertext: theory into practice, MacAleese, R. (ed). Oxford: Blackwell.

Barrett, E. (ed) (1988) - Text, Context, and Hypertext. Cambridge, Mass.: MIT Press.

Benest, I.D., Morgan, G. and Smithurst, M.D. (1987) - "A Humanized Interface to an Electronic Library". In Proceedings of Interact '87, Bullinger, H. J. and Shackel, B. (eds). Amsterdam: Elsevier Science.

Bobrow, D.G., Kaplan, R.M., Kay, M., Norman, D.A., Thompson, H. and Winograd, T. (1977) - "GUS, A Frame-Driven Dialog System". Artificial Intelligence, 8, 155-173.

Borgman, C.L. (1984) - "The user's mental model of an information retrieval system: Effects on performance". Unpublished PhD Thesis, Stanford University.

Borgman, C.L. (1986a) - "The User's Mental Model of an Information Retrieval System: An Experiment on a Prototype On-Line Catalog". International Journal of Man-Machine Studies, 24, 47-64.

Borgman, C.L. (1986b) - "Why are online catalogs so hard to use? Lessons learned from information-retrieval studies". Journal of the American Society for Information Science, 37, 387-400.

Brand, S. (1987) - The Media Lab: Inventing the Future at MIT. New York: Viking Penguin.

Brod, C. (1984) - Technostress: The Human Cost of the Computer Revolution. Reading, Mass.: Addison-Wesley.

Brooks, F.P. Jr (1988) - "Grasping Reality Through Illusion - Interactive Graphics Serving Science". In Proceedings of CHI'88, Conference on Human Factors in Computing Systems. New York: ACM.

Brown, C.M. (1986) - Human-Computer Interface Design Guidelines. Norwood, NJ: Ablex.

Card, S.K. and Henderson, A.H. Jr. (1987) - "A Multiple, Virtual-Workspace Interface to Support User Task Switching". In Proceedings of CHI and GI 1987, Conference on Human Factors in Computing Systems and Graphics Interface. New York: Association for Computing Machinery.

Card, S.K., English, W.K. and Burr, B.J. (1978) - "Evaluation of mouse, rate-controlled isometric joystick, step keys, and text keys for selection on a CRT". Ergonomics, 21, 601-613.

Cardwell, G.F. (1987) - "A Good Interface is Difficult to Design". Computer Graphics (1987).

Carlson, D.A. and Ram, S. (1990) - "HyperIntelligence: The Next Frontier". Communications of the ACM, 33, 311-321.

Caroll, J.M. and Mack, R.L. (1985) - "Metaphor, computing systems, and active learning". International Journal of Man-Machine Studies, 22, 39-57.

Caroll, J.M. and Thomas, J.C. (1982) - "Metaphor and the Cognitive Representation of Computing Systems". IEEE Transactions on Systems, Man and Cybernetics, 12, 107-182.

Carroll, J.M., Mack, R.L. and Kellogg, W.A. (1988) - "Interface Metaphors and User Interface Design". In M Helander (ed), Handbook of Human-Computer Interaction. Amsterdam: North-Holland.

Carter, J.A. (1986) - "A taxonomy of user-oriented functions". International Journal of Man-Machine Studies, 24, 195-292.

Cheriton, D.R. (1976) - "Man-machine interface for time-sharing systems". Proceedings of the ACM National Conference, 362-380.

Chignell, M.H. (1989) - "Visualization and Navigation in Hypermedia". Unpublished manuscript. Department of Industrial and Systems Engineering, University of Southern California, Los Angeles.

Chignell, M.H. and Lacy, R.M. (1988) - "Integrating research and instruction: Project Jefferson". Academic Computer, September, 1988.

Chignell, M.H., Hancock, P.A. and Loewenthal, A. (eds) (1986) - Interfaces: Theory, Research, and Design. Amsterdam: North Holland.

Chignell, M.H.,Valdez, J.F. and Waterworth, J.A. (1991)- "Knowledge Engineering for Hypermedia". In J.A. Waterworth (ed), Multimedia: technology and applications. Chichester: Ellis Horwood..

Chignell, M.H., Nordhausen, B., Valdez, J.F. and Waterworth, J.A. (in press). "Project HEFTI: Hypertext Extraction From Text Incrementally". Hypermedia journal.

Chua, T.S. and Lai, E.P.M. (1991)- "Composition Editor for Hypermedia Environment". In J.A. Waterworth (ed), Multimedia: technology and applications. Chichester, UK: Ellis Horwood.

Collins COBUILD English Language Dictionary (1987). London: Collins.

Conklin, J. (1987) - "Hypertext: A Survey and Introduction". IEEE Computer, 20, 9, 17-41.

Conklin, J. and Begeman, M.L. (1987) - "gIBIS: A hypertext tool for team design deliberation". Proceedings of Hypertext '87, Chapel Hill, NC.

Croft, W.B. (1987) - "Approaches to intelligent information retrieval". Information Processing and Management, 23, 249-254.

Cuomo, D.L. and Sharit, J. (1989) - "A Study of Human Performance in Computer-Aided Architectural Design". International Journal Of Human-Computer Interaction, 1, 69-107.

Diaper, D (1986) - "Identifying the Knowledge Requirements of an Expert System's Natural Language Processing Interface". In M D Harrison and A F Monk (eds.), People and Computer II. Cambridge University Press.

Diaper, D and Winder, R (1987) - People and Computers III. Cambridge University Press.

Douglas, S.A. and Moran, T.P. (1983) - "Learning Text Editor Semantics by Analogy". Proceedings of CHI'83, 207-211.

Dumas, J. (1988) - Designing User Interfaces for Software. Englewood Cliffs, NJ, USA: Prentice Hall.

Eberts, R. (1987) - "Human-Computer Interaction". In P.A. Hancock (ed.), Human Factors Psychology. Amsterdam, North-Holland.

Edmonds, E. A., and Guest, S. P. (1984) - "The SYNICS2 user interface manager". In Proceedings of INTERACT 84, 1st IFIP Conference on Human-Computer Interaction, vol. 1, 53-56.

Edmondson, W. (1989) - "Asynchronous parallelism in human behaviour: a cognitive science perspective on human-computer interaction". Behaviour and Information Technology, 8, 3-12.

Egan, D.E., Remde, J.R., Landauer, T.K., Lochbaum, C.C. and Gomez, L.M. (1989) - "Behavioral Evaluation and Analysis of a Hypertext Browser". In Proceedings of CHI'89, Conference on Human Factors in Computing Systems. New York: ACM.

Ellis, D. (1989) "A behavioural approach to information retrieval system design". Journal of Documentation, 45, 171-212.

Engelbart, D.C. and English, W.K. (1968) - "A Research Centre for Augmenting Human Intellect". AFIPS Conference Proceedings, 33(1) Washington DC: Thompson Book Company.

Erickson, T.D. (1989) - "Interfaces for Cooperative Work: An Eclectic Look at CSCW '88". ACM SIGCHI Bulletin, 21, 1, 56-64.

Erlich, W.R. and Williges, R.C. (eds) (1986) - Human-Computer Dialogue Design. Amsterdam: Elsevier.

Ewing, J., Mehrabanzad, S., Sheck, S., Ostroff, D. and Shneiderman, B. (1986) - "An experimental comparison of a mouse and arrow-jump keys for an interactive encyclopedia". International Journal of Man-Machine Studies, 24, 29-45.

Fairchild, K.M., Poltrock, S.E. and Furnas, G.W. (1988) - "SemNet: Three-Dimensional Graphics Representations of Large Knowledge Bases". In Cognitive Science and its Applications for Human-Computer Interaction, R. Guindon (ed). Hillsdale NJ: Lawrence Erlbaum Associates.

Fairchild, K.M., Meredith, G. and Wexelblat, A. (1989) - "The Tourist Artificial Reality". Proceedings of CHI'89, Conference on Human Factors in Computing Systems. New York: ACM.

Fischer, G. and Lemke, A.C. (1988) - "Construction Kits and Design Environments: Steps Toward Human Problem-Domain Communication". Human-Computer Interaction, 3, 179-222.

Fisher, G.L. and Joy K.I. (1987) - "A Control Panel Interface for Graphics and Image Processing Applications". In Proceedings of CHI and GI 1987, Conference on Human Factors in Computing Systems and Graphics Interface. New York: Association for Computing Machinery.

Fitter, M. (1979) - "Towards more "natural" interactive systems". International Journal of Man-Machine Studies, 11, 339-350.

Foley, J.D. (1987) - "Interfaces for Advanced Computing". Scientific American, 257(4), 82-90.

Foley, J.D, Gibbs, C., Kim, W.C. and Kovacevic, S. (1988) - "A Knowledge-Based User Interface Management System". In Proceedings of CHI'88, Conference on Human Factors in Computing Systems. New York: ACM.

Frisse, M.E. (1988) - "Searching for Information in a Hypermedia Medical Handbook". Communications of the ACM, 31, 880-886.

Gaines, B.R. and Facey, P.V. (1975) - "Some experience in interactive system development and application". Proceedings of IEEE, 63, 894-911.

Gaines, B.R. and Shaw, M.L.G. (1983) - "Dialogue Engineering". In Designing for Human-Computer Communication, M.E. Sime and M.J. Coombs (eds.), London: Academic.

Galitz, W.O. (1985) - Handbook of Screen Format Design. Amsterdam: North-Holland.

Gardner, M. and Christie, B. (eds) (1987) - Applying Cognitive Psychology to User Interface Design. Chichester, UK: Wiley.

Gebhardt, F. and Stellmacher, I. (1978) - "Design criteria for document retrieval languages". Journal of the American Society for Information Science, 29, 191-199.

Gittens, D. (1986) - "Icon-based human-computer interaction". International Journal of Man-Machine Studies, 24, 519-543.

Grice, A.P. (1975) - "Logic and Conversation". In Syntax and Semantics III: Speech Acts, P. Cole and J.L. Morgan (eds.), New York and London: Academic.

Guindon, R. (1988) - "How to interface to advisory systems?: users request help with a very simple language". Proceedings of CHI'88, Conference on Human Factors in Computing Systems. New York: ACM.

Gullichsen, E. and Fairchild, K.M. (1987) - "The Modern Alchemists". Proceedings of 1987 Workshop on Visual Languages, August 19-21, Linkoping, Sweden, 348-364.

Halasz, F.G. (1987) - "NoteCards in a Nutshell". Proceedings of CHI + GI' 87, Conference on Human Factors in Computing Systems. New York: ACM.

Halasz, F.G. (1988) - "Reflections on Notecards: seven issues for the next generation of hypermedia systems". Communications of the ACM, 31, 836-852.

Halasz, F.G. and Moran, T.P. (1982) - "Analogy considered harmful". Proceedings of the Conference on Human Factors in Computing Systems, Gaithersburg, Maryland USA.

Halasz, F.G, Moran, T. and Trigg, R. (1987) - "Notecards in a Nutshell". Proceedings of CHI and GI'87 Conference on Human Factors in Computing Systems and Graphics Interfaces. New York: ACM.

Hammond, N. and Allinson, L. (1987) - "The Travel Metaphor as Design Principle and Training Aid for Navigating around Complex Systems. In D. Diaper and R. Winder (eds.), People and Computers III Cambridge: Cambridge University Press.

Hammond, N. and Allinson, L. (1988) - "Travels around a learning support environment: Rambling, orienteering or touring". CHI'88 Proceedings, pp. 269-273. Conference on Human Factors in Computing Systems. New York: ACM.

Hansen, W.J. (1971) - "User engineering principles for interactive systems". Proceedings of the Fall Joint Computer Conference, 39, 523-532. Montvale, NJ: AFIPS Press.

Hanusa, H. (1983) - "Tools and techniques for the monitoring of interactive graphics dialogues". International Journal of Man-Machine Studies, 19, 163-180.

Hardman, L. (1989) - "Evaluating the usability of the Glasgow online hypertext." Hypermedia, 1 34-63.

Hartson, H.R. (ed) (1985 and 1987) - Advances in Human-Computer Interaction, Volumes I and II. Norwood, New Jersey: Ablex.

Hartson, H.R. and Johnson, D.H. (1983) - "Dialogue Management: New Concepts in Human-Computer Interface Development". Technical Report CSIE-83-13, Office of Naval Research, Code 442, 800 North Quincey Street, Arlington VA 22217, USA.

Hashimoto, O. and Miyai, H. (1987) - "INTERA/P: A User Interface Prototyping Tool". In Diaper, D. and Winder R. (eds), People and Computers III. Cambridge: Cambridge University Press.

Hayes, P.J. and Reddy, R. (1983) - "Steps toward graceful interaction in spoken and written man-machine communication". International Journal of Man-Machine Studies, 19, 231-284.

Hayes, P.J. and Szekely (1983) - "Graceful interaction through the COUSIN Command Interface". International Journal of Man-Machine Studies, 19, 285-305.

Henderson, D.A. (1986) - "The Trillium User Interface Design Environment". Proceedings of CHI 86, Conference on Human Factors in Computing Systems, 221-227. New York: ACM.

Heppe, D.L., Edmondson, W.H. and Spence, R.(1985) - "Helping both the novice and the advanced user in menu-driven information retrieval systems". In P. Johnson and S. Cook (eds.), People and Computers. Cambridge: Cambridge University Press.

Hirshheim, R.A. (1985) - Office Automation: A Social and Organizational Perspective. Chichester, UK: Wiley.

Hoey, M. (1983) - On the Surface of Discourse. Oxford: Oxford University Press.

Hutchins, E.L. (1989) - "Metaphors for Interface Design". In D.G. Bouwhis, M.M. Taylor and F. Neel (eds.), The Structure of Multimodal Dialogue, Amsterdam: North Holland.

Hutchins, E.L., Hollan, J.D. and Norman, D.A. (1986) - "Direct Manipulation Interfaces. In D.A. Norman and S.W. Draper (eds), User Centered System Design. Hillsdale, NJ: Lawrence Erlbaum Associates.

Jacob, R. (1985) - "An Executable Specification Technique for Describing Human-Computer Interaction. In Hartson, H. (ed), Advances in Human-Computer Interaction, NJ: Ablex.

Johnson-Laird, P.N. (1983) - Mental Models. Cambridge, Mass.: Harvard University Press.

Jones, M.K. - Human-Computer Interaction: a design guide. Englewood Cliffs, NJ, USA: Educational Technology Publications.

Jones, W.P. (1986) - "The Memory Extender Personal Filing System". Proceedings of CHI'86, Conference on Human Factors in Computing Systems. New York: ACM.

Jones, W.P. (1987) - "How Do We Distinguish the Hyper from the Hype in Non-linear Text ?". In D. Bullinger and B. Shackel (eds.), Proceedings of Interact'87. Amsterdam: Elsevier Science.

Jones, W.P. (1989) - "As We May Think?: Psychological considerations in the design of a personal filing system". In Guindon, R (ed), Cognitive Science and its Applications for Human-Computer Interaction. Lawrence Erlbaum Associates.

Jones, W.P. and Dumais, S. (1986) - "The Spatial Metaphor for User Interfaces: Experimental Test of Reference by Location versus Naming". ACM Transactions on Office Information Systems, 4, 42-63.

Kahn, P. and Meyrowitz, N. (1988) - "Guide, HyperCard, and Intermedia: A Comparison of Hypertext/Hypermedia Systems". Unpublished draft manuscript (August 12, 1988), Institute for Research in Information and Scholarship, Brown University.

Kelly, M.J. and Chapanis, A. (1977) - "Limited vocabulary natural language dialog". International Journal of Man-Machine Studies, 9, 477-501.

Kennedy, T.C.S. (1974) - "The design of interactive procedures for man-machine communication", International Journal of Man-Machine Studies, 6, 309-334.

Koh, T.T. and Chua, T.S. (1989) - "On the Design of a Frame-Based Hypermedia System". In Hypertext: theory into practice, MacAleese, R. (ed). Oxford: Blackwell.

Krueger, M.W. (1991) - Artificial Reality II. Reading, Mass.: Addison-Wesley.

Laurel, B. (ed) (1990) - The Art of Human-Computer Interface Design. Reading, Mass., USA: Addison-Wesley.

Levinson, S.C. (1983) - Pragmatics. Cambridge: Cambridge University Press.

Lewis, C. (1982) - "Using the "thinking aloud" method in cognitive interface design". IBM Research Report RC-9265, Yorktown Heights, NY.

Loo, J.P.L. and Chung, T.M. (1991) - "An Environment for Evaluating Browsing in Hypermedia Systems". Presented at IFIP WG9.1: Human Job and Computer Interfaces Conference, Finland, August 1991.

Lowe, D.G. (1985) - "Cooperative structure of information: The representation of reasoning and debate". International Journal of Man-Machine Studies, 23, 97-111.

Lowgren, J. (1988) - "History, State, and Future of User Interface Management Systems". SIGCHI Bulletin, 20, 32-44.

Macmillan, S.A. (1984) - "User Models to Personalize an Intelligent Agent". PhD thesis, Stanford University.

Malone, T.W. (1988) - "Computer Supported Cooperative Work: Using Information Technology for Coordination". User Interface Strategies '88 (Videos of a two-day satellite TV course). Produced by Instructional Television System.

Malone, T.W. et al (1986) - "Semi-Structured Messages are Surprisingly Useful for Computer-Supported Coordination". Proceedings of the Conference on Computer-Supported Cooperative Work, Austin Texas, December 1986.

Mantei, M. (1982) - "Disorientation behavior in person-computer interaction". Ph.D. Dissertation, University of Southern California.

Maguire, M. (1982) - "An evaluation of published recommendations on the design of man-computer dialogues". International Journal of Man-Machine Studies, 16, 237-261.

Marchionini, G. and Shneiderman B. (1988) - "Finding Facts vs. Browsing Knowledge in Hypertext Systems". IEEE Computer, Jan, 70-80.

Marcus, A. (1983) - "Graphic design for computer graphics". IEEE Computer Graphics and Applications, July, 63-70.

Mayer R. E. (1981)- The Promise of Cognitive Psychology. San Francisco: Freeman.

McKnight, C., Dillon, A. and Richardson, J. (1989) - "A Comparison of Linear and Hypertext Formats in Information Retrieval". In Proceedings of Hypertext 2, University of York, UK, June 1989.

Miller, G.A. (1956) - "The magical number seven, plus or minus two: some limits on our capacity for processing information". Psychological Review, 63, 81-97.

Minsky, M. (1975) - "A Framework for Representing Knowledge". In Winston, P. (ed.) The Psychology of Computer Vision. New York: MacGraw-Hill, pp 211-277.

Monk, A.F. (1989) - "Getting to Known Locations in a Hypertext". In Proceedings of Hypertext 2, University of York, UK, June 1989.

Monk, A.F., Walsh, P. and Dix, A.J. (1988) - "A comparison of hypertext, scrolling, and folding". In R. Winder (ed.), People and Computers IV, Proceedings of HCI'88. Cambridge: Cambridge University Press.

Murray, D. and Bevan, N. (1984) - "The Social Psychology of Computer Conversations". In Proceedings of Interact'84, B. Shackel (ed). Amsterdam: Elsevier Science.

Myers, B.A. (1987a) - "Creating Dynamic Interaction Techniques by Demonstration". In Proceedings of CHI and GI 1987, Conference on Human Factors in Computing Systems and Graphics Interface. New York: Association for Computing Machinery.

Myers , B.A. (1987b) - "Gaining General Acceptance for UIMS". Computer Graphics, 21 (2).

Myers, B.A. (1989) - "User Interface Tools: Introduction and Survey". IEEE Software, 15-23, January 1989.

Negroponte, N. (1989) - "An Iconoclastic View Beyond the Desktop Metaphor". International Journal Of Human-Computer Interaction, 1, 109-113.

Nelson, T. H. (1990) - "The Right Way to Think About Software Design". In B. Laurel (ed), The Art of Human-Computer Interface Design. Reading, Mass: Addison-Wesley.

Nielsen, J. (1990a) - "The Art of Navigating through Hypertext". Communications of the ACM, 33, 297-310.

Nielsen, J. (1990b) - Hypertext and Hypermedia. New York: Academic.

Nielsen, J. (1990c) - Contribution to "Evaluating Hypermedia Systems". Panel session in Proceedings of CHI'90. New York: ACM.

Nielsen, J. and Lyngbaek, U. (1989) - "Two Field Studies of Hypermedia usability". In Proceedings of Hypertext 2, University of York, UK, June 1989.

Nordhausen, B., Chignell, M.H. and Waterworth, J.A. (1991) - "The Missing Link? Comparison of Manual and Automated Linking in Hypertext Engineering". In Proceedings of the 35th Annual Meeting of the Human Factors Society, San Francisco, August 1991.

Norman, D.A. and Draper, S.D. (1986) - User Centered System Design. Lawrence Erlbaum.

Norman, D.A. and Rumelhart, D. (1975) - Explorations in Cognition. San Francisco: Freeman.

Ochsman, R.B. and Chapanis, A. (1974) - "The effects of ten communication modes on the behavior of teams during cooperative problem-solving". International Journal of Man-Machine Studies, 6, 579-619.

Olsen, D. (1986) - "MIKE: Menu Interaction Kontrol Environment". ACM Transactions on Graphics, 5 (4), 318-344.

Olsen, D. and Dempsey, E. (1983) - "SYNGRAPH: A Graphic User Interface Generator". Computer Graphics, 17:3.

Parsaye, K., Chignell, M.H., Khoshafian, S., and Wong, H.K.T. (1989) - Intelligent Databases: Object-Oriented, Deductive Hypermedia Technologies. N.Y.: Wiley.

Patterson, D. (1990) - Introduction to Artificial Intelligence and Expert Systems. Englewood Cliffs, NJ: Prentice Hall.

Payne, S. (1987) - "Complex Problem Spaces: Modelling the Knowledge Needed to Use Interactive Devices". In D. Bullinger and B. Shackel (eds.), Proceedings of Interact'87 Amsterdam: Elsevier Science.

Peckham, J.B. (1984) - "Speech Recognition - What is it worth?". In Proceedings of the First International Conference on Speech Technology. Bedford, UK: IFS.

Pew, R.W. and Rollins, A.M. (1975) - Report No. 3129, Bolt, Beranek and Newman. Cambridge, Massachusetts.

Press, L. (1971) - "Toward balanced man-machine systems". International Journal of Man-Machine Studies, 3, 61-73.

Rada, R. and Barlow, J (1988) - "Expert Systems and Hypertext". The Knowledge Engineering Review, 3, 285-302.

Reichman, R. (1985) - Getting computers to talk like you and me. Cambridge, Mass.: MIT Press.

Reisner, P. (1981) - "Formal Grammar and Human Factors Design of an Interactive Graphics System". IEEE Transactions on Software Engineering SE-7, 2, 229-240.

Rich, E. (1984) - "Natural Language Interaction". IEEE Computer, September.

Ronnquist, R. (1984) - "Customising Command Language Dialogues with the YAKI Package". ASLAB Memo 84-03, University of Linkoping, Sweden.

Rosch, E., and Mervis, C.B. (1975) - "Family resemblances: Studies in the internal structure of categories". Cognitive Psychology, 7, 573-605.

Rosch, E., Mervis, C.B., Gray, W.D., Johnson, D.M., and Boyes-Bream, P. (1976) - "Basic objects in natural categories". Cognitive Psychology, 8, 382-439.

Rumelhart, D.E. and McLelland, J.L. (eds.) (1986) - Parallel Distributed Processing: Explorations in the Microstructure of Cognition. Vol I. Cambridge, Mass.: MIT Press.

Rumelhart, D.E. and Norman, D.A. (1983) - "Analogical Processes in Learning". In J.R. Anderson (ed.) Cognitive Skills and their Acquisition. Hillsdale, NJ: Lawrence Erlbaum Associates.

Salomon, G., Oren, T., and Kreitman, K. (1989) - "Using guides to explore multimedia databases". In Proceedings of the 22nd Annual Hawaii International Conference on Systems Sciences, Volume III, pp. 3-12.

Salton, G. (1989) - Automatic Text Processing: The Transformation, Analysis, and Retrieval of Information by Computer. Reading, Mass.: Addison-Wesley.

Salton, G. and McGill, M.J. (1983) - Introduction to modern information retrieval. New York: McGraw-Hill.

Scapin, D.L. (1981) - "Computer commands in restricted natural language: Some aspects of memory and experience." Human Factors, 23, 365-375.

Schegloff, E. and Sacks, H.(1973) - "Opening up closings". Semiotica, 8, 289-327.

Schmucker, K.J. (1986) - "MacApp: An Application Framework". Byte, August, 189-192.

Schulert, A.J., Rogers, G.T., and Hamilton, J.A. (1985) - "ADM - A Dialog Manager". In Proceedings of CHI'85, Conference on Human Factors in Computer Systems. New York: Association for Computing Machinery.

Searle, J.R. (1969) - Speech Acts. Cambridge: Cambridge University Press.

Sharratt, B. (1987) - "The Incorporation of Early Interface Evaluation into Command Language Grammar Specification". In Diaper, D and Winder, R - People and Computers III. Cambridge: Cambridge University Press.

Shneiderman, B. (1982) - "System Message Design". In Badre and Shneiderman (eds), Directions in Human/Computer Interaction. Norwood, NJ: Ablex.

Shneiderman, B. (1987a) - Designing the User Interface: Strategies for Effective Human-Computer Interaction. Reading, Mass.: Addison-Wesley.

Shneiderman, B. (1987b) - "User interface design for the HyperTies electronic encyclopedia". Proceedings of Hypertext'87, Chapel Hill, North Carolina.

Shneiderman, B. (1989) - "Evaluating Three Museum Installations of a Hypertext System". Journal of the American Society for Information Science, 40, 172-182..

Shotton, M.A. (1989) - Computer Addiction? - A Study of Computer Dependency. London: Taylor and Francis.

Shute, S.J., Smith, P.J., Krawczak, D.A., Chignell, M.H., and Sater, M. (1986) - "Enhancing cognitive compatibility in a knowledge-based information retrieval system". In 1986 Fall Industrial Engineering Conference Proceedings, pp. 111-115.

Simon, H.A. (1981) - The Sciences of the Artificial. Cambridge, Mass.: MIT Press.

Simpson, A. and McKnight, C. (1989) - "Navigation in Hypertext: Structural Cues and Mental Maps". In Proceedings of Hypertext 2, University of York, UK, June 1989.

Singh, G. (1991) - "UIMS Support for Multimedia User Interfaces". In J. A. Waterworth, (ed.), Multimedia: technology and applications. Chichester, UK: Ellis Horwood..

Singh, G. and Green, M. (1988) - "Designing the Interface Designer's Interface". In Proceedings of ACM SIGGRAPH Symposium on User Interface Software. New York: ACM.

Singh, G., Kok, C.H. and Ngan T.Y. (1990) - "Druid: A System for Demonstrational Rapid User Interface Development". Proceedings of UIST'90. New York: ACM.

Smith, R.B. (1987) - "Experiences with Alternative Reality Kit: An Example of the Tension Between Literalism and Magic". IEEE Computer Graphics and Applications, 7, 42-50.

Sperber, D. and Wilson, D. (1986) - Relevance. Oxford: Basil Blackwell.

Sperling, G. (1960) - "The information available in brief visual presentations". Psychological Monographs, 74, whole no. 498.

Streitz, N.A., Hannemann, J.and Thuring, M. (1989) - "From Ideas and Arguments to Hyperdocuments: Travelling through Activity Spaces". In Hypertext'89 Proceedings. New York: ACM.

Taylor, M.M. (1989) - "Response Timing in Layered Protocols: A Cybernetic View of Natural Dialogue". In M.M .Taylor, F. Neel and D.G. Bouwhuis (eds), The Structure of Multimodal Dialogue. Amsterdam: North-Holland.

Taylor, M.M., Neel, F. and Bouwhuis, D.G. (eds) (1989) - The Structure of Multimodal Dialogue. Amsterdam: North-Holland.

Thimbleby, H. (1980) - "Dialogue Determination". International Journal of Man-Machine Studies, 13, 295-304.

Thimbleby, H. (1984) - "User Interface Design: Generative User Engineering Principles". In Fundamentals of Human-Computer Interaction (ed Monk, A., Academic Press).

Thomas, C. (1987) - "Designing Electronic Paper to Fit User Requirements". In People and Computers III (eds Diaper & Winder, Cambridge University Press).

Thompson, R.H. and Croft, W.B. (1989) - "Support for browsing in an intelligent text retrieval system". International Journal of Man-Machine Studies, 30, 639-668.

Tombaugh, J.W. and McEwen, S.A. (1982) - "Comparison of two information retrieval methods on Videotex: Tree-structure versus alphabetic directory". Proceedings of Human Factors in Computer Systems, 1982, pp. 106-110.

Tong, R.M. (1987) - "Conceptual Information Retrieval using RUBRIC". Proceedings of ACM SIGIR Conference on R&D in Information Retrieval. New York: ACM.

Trigg, R.H. and Irish, P.M. (1987) - "Hypertext habitats: Experiences of writers in NoteCards". Proceedings of Hypertext '87, Chapel Hill, NC.

Turoff, M., Whitescarver, J. and Hiltz, S.R. (1978) - "The human machine interface in a computerized conferencing environment". Proceedings of IEEE Conference on Interactive Systems, Man, and Cybernetics, 145-157.

Valdez, J.F., Chignell, M.H., and Glenn, B. (1988) - "Browsing models for hypermedia databases". Proceedings of the Annual Meeting of the Human Factors Society.

Vertelney, L (1989) - Contribution to Panel on "Drama and Personality in User Interface Design". Proceedings of CHI'89, Conference on Human Factors in Computer Systems. New York: Association for Computing Machinery.

Wang, X. and Chua, T.S. (1990) - "Support for Search and Dynamic Linking in a Hypertext Environment". Internal Report, Institute of Systems Science, National University of Singapore.

Wasserman, A. (1973) - "The design of idiot-proof interactive systems". Proceedings of the National Computer Conference, 42. Montvale, NJ: AFIPS Press.

Wasserman, A. and Shewmake, D. (1985) - "The Role of Prototypes in the User Software Engineering (USE) Methodology". In Hartson, H. (ed), Advances in Human-Computer Interaction, NJ: Ablex.

Waterworth, J.A. (1982) - "Man-machine speech 'dialogue acts'". Applied Ergonomics, 13, 203-207.

Waterworth, J.A. (1984) - "Interaction with Machines by Voice: a Telecommunications Perspective". Behaviour and Information Technology, 3, 163-177.

Waterworth, J.A. (1989) - "Interactive Strategies for Conversational Computer Systems". In M.M. Taylor, F. Neel and D.G. Bouwhuis (eds), The Structure of Multimodal Dialogue. Amsterdam: North-Holland.

Waterworth, J.A. (ed.) (1991), Multimedia: technology and applications. Chichester, UK: Ellis Horwood..

Waterworth, J.A. and Chignell, M.H. (1989a) - "A Manifesto for Hypermedia Usability Research". Hypermedia, 1, 205-234.

Waterworth, J.A. and Chignell, M.H. (1989b) - "Dimensions of Hypermedia Usability". Working Paper WP89-07-0, Institute of Systems Science, National University of Singapore.

Waterworth, J.A. and Chignell, M.H. (1991) - "A Model of Information Exploration". Hypermedia, 3, 35-58.

Waterworth, J.A. and Talbot, M (1987) - Speech- and Language-Based Interaction with Machines. Chichester, UK: Ellis Horwood.

Weyer, S.A. (1982) - "The design of a dynamic book for information search". International Journal of Man-Machine Studies, 17, 87-107.

Weyer, S.A. and Borning, J. (1985) - "A Prototype Electronic Encyclopedia". ACM Transactions on Office Information Systems, 3, 63-88.

Whalen, T. and Patrick, A. (1989) - "Conversational Hypertext: Information Access through Natural Language Dialogues with Computers". Proceedings of CHI'89, Conference on Human Factors in Computer Systems, 289-292. New York: ACM .

Whiteside, J., Bennett, J. and Holtzblatt, K. (1988) - "Usability Engineering: Our Experience and Evolution". In M. Helander, Handbook of Human-Computer Interaction. Amsterdam: Elsevier.

Winograd, T. (1979) - "Beyond Programming Languages". Communications of the ACM, 22, 391-401.

Winograd, T. and Flores F. (1986) - Understanding Computers and Cognition: A New Foundation for Design. Norwood, NJ: Ablex.

Wright, P., and Lickorish, A. (1989) - "An empirical study of two navigation systems for two hypertexts". Proceedings of Hypertext 2, University of York, UK, June 1989.

Yankelovich, N., Meyrowitz, N. and van Dam, A. (1985) - "Reading and Writing the Electronic Book". IEEE Computer, October, 1985.

Yankelovich, N., Haan, B., and Meyrowitz, N. (1988) - "Intermedia: The concept and the construction of a seamless information environment". IEEE Computer (January, 1989).

Yoder, E., Akscyn, R. and McCracken, D. (1989) - "Collaboration in KMS, A Shared Hypermedia System". Proceedings of CHI'89, Conference on Human Factors in Computing Systems. New York: ACM.

Zimmerman, R (1977) - Personal communication, reported in Bailey (1982).

Index

accessibility of information, 186
actions, 33
adaptive change, 97
adventure games, 92, 185
agents, 184
Alternative Reality Kit, 25
Alty, 57, 140
analogy, 88
anthropometric research, 79
anthropomorphic approach, 81
Apple, 59
architecture, 50
argumentation stuctures, 101
attention,, 37
automated icon, 84
automatic linking, 160

Bailey, 59
Baird and Percival, 106
Barrett, 84
Beckett, 19
behavioural trials, 41
behaviours, 33
Benest, 93
black art of interface design, 60, 92
Bobrow, 22
book-like hypertext, 76
Borgman, 70, 86, 90, 122
Brod, 175, 185
Brooks, 25

Brown, 57
browse, 75, 114, 159
   -encouraging' questions, 125
Burnt Norton, 174

CAL, 112
Calvino, 50
Card, 79
Card and Henderson, 24, 89
Cardwell, 63
Carroll, 88
case studies, 140
chaining, 134
channel of communication, 33
Cheriton, 59
chess, 23
Chignell, 71, 83, 85, 113, 159
Chignell and Lacy, 73
Christian art, 120
cities
   city planning, 52
   Information City, 178
   Invisible Cities, 50
   landmarks, 85, 180
   map of the city, 180
   Sci-fi Village, 182
   size of a building, 180
classification of design tools, 67
COBUILD, 114, 126
cognitive psychology, 32

collaborative work, 101
command languages, 68
  command menus, 129
components, 149
computer literacy, 175, 183
Computer-Aided Instruction
  (CAI), 77, 140
conceptual
  analysis, 56
  model, 91
  structure, 78
Conklin and Begeman, 73
Conklin, 101
connectivity, 85
consciousness, 35
consistency, 38
construction kits, 66
Contexts, 33
conversation
  conversational analysis, 82
  and discourse analysis, 57
  conversational hypertext, 83
  and interaction, 79, 81
Coordinator, 101
creating an interaction model, 56
credibility, 149
Cuomo and Sharit, 42

decontextualization of knowledge,
  184
dehumanization, 185
democratization of access to
  knowledge, 186
demonstrational model, 66
design
  environments, 68
  guidelines, 57
  recommendations, 146, 156
dialogue
  authors, 62
  dialogue level analysis, 56
Diaper, 62
differentiation, 134
direct manipulation, 69, 89
directed navigation, 80
discovery-based information
  exploration, 116

displays, 33
documentation, 101
dogmas, 177
Druid, 66
dynamic hypermedia, 97

Eberts, 79, 81
ecological validity, 74
Edmonds and Guest, 63
Edmondson, 82
effects, 33
Egan, 74, 101
egyptology, 51
electronic media
  discussions, 187
  electronic mail, 186
Eliot, 174
Ellis, 114, 133
embeddedness, 27
empirical studies of hypermedia
  usability, 74
entertainment, 127, 185
Erickson, 186
evaluation, 41
  evaluated relevance, 160
Ewing, 79
examples of information
  exploration, 118
experiment, 43
  comparison of 4 styles, 123
  psychology and HCI, 32
experts, 180
  expert assessment, 143, 180
exploratory navigation, 80
external factors, 93
extracting and evaluating, 135
extrinsic menus, 130

Fairchild, 80, 83, 84
fakes, 61
feedback, 38
filters for particular users and
  types of tasks, 86
Fischer and Lemke, 66
Fisher and Joy, 63
Fitter, 81
flexibility, 38, 77

floor plans, 109
Florence, 121
Foley, 68, 80
forgetting, 86
forms, 33
   form filling, 68
formative evaluation, 143
frequency, 86
Friday the 13th, 185
Frisse, 131, 132
functionality and intelligibility, 100
future hypermedia systems, 94

Gaines and Facey, 59
Gaines and Shaw, 59
gateway, 129
Gebhardt and Stellmacher, 59
genetic engineering, 175
gIBIS, 101
Glasgow Online, 106
global evaluation, 159
goals, 33
   goals and subgoals, 49
gracefulness, 81
grammars, 64
Grice, 59
Guindon, 82

Halasz, 26, 74, 83, 94
Halasz and Moran, 24, 90, 94
halo effect, 143
Hammond and Allinson, 74, 92,
   93, 102
Hansen, 59
Hardman, 74
Haroun and the Sea of Stories, 71
Hartson and Johnson, 62
Hayes, 62
Hayes and Reddy, 81
HEFTI, 159, 161
help module, 152
Heppe, 76
heresies and dogmas, 176
heterogeneous information, 78
hierarchical organization of
   information, 76
history, 50

history of ideas, 184
hitchhiker metaphor, 102
Hoey, 85
holiday, 178
home videos, 186
hostess, 178
human factors, 21
   specialists, 62
human information processing, 34
human-human communication, 81
Hutchins, 69, 73, 82, 90
hypermedia, 72
   mayhem of the 1990s, 100
   Hypertext on Hypertext, 123
   Hypertext'87, 123
   hypertization, 141

I^3R, 132
immediate store (IS), 34
importance, 85
indexing
   index linking, 131
   indexing, 99
inference, 99
information
   information 'filters', 96
   information artefacts, 187
   Information City, 178
   information exploration, 114
   exploration systems, 127
   information retrieval, 73, 113
intelligent tutor, 141
interaction
   interaction method, 117
   interaction modes, 91
   interactive encyclopaedia, 79
   interactive fiction, 127
   interactivity, 20
interface specification, 65
interviews, 50
intrinsic menus, 130
Invisible Cities, 50
Islamic Art, 122
isomorphism, 32
iterative cycle of design,, 31
iterative development, 60
Iyer, 174

Jacob, 63
Japanese occupation of Singapore,
  98
Jason, 185
Jones, 84, 86, 112
jukebox icon, 106

karaoke, 183
Kelly and Chapanis, 81
Kennedy, 59
keywords, 86
Koh and Chua, 92, 98
Krueger, 177, 185

landmarks, 85, 180
lecturing, 53
Leonardo da Vinci, 121
Levinson, 57
Lewis, 42
lexical analysis, 56
liberalization, 183
library-like representation, 93
linguistics, 57
link, 127
literacy, 183
literal features, 93
locus of evaluation, 46
long term store (LTS), 35
Loo and Chung, 106
lost in spaghetti, 72
Lowgren, 64

magic aspects, 93
  magic corridors, 180
Maguire, 59
Majulah Singapura, 106
Mantei, 73
manual linking, 160, 161
map of the city, 180
Marchionini and Shneiderman, 74
Marcus, 57
Mayer, 32
McKnight, 74, 130
mediacy, 183
mediated browsing, 118
mediated querying, 118
mental models, 91

menu selection, 68
meta-information, 82
metaphor, 88, 91, 92
metrics, 41
Michelangelo, 120
Miller, 35
mind experiments, 61
monitoring, 135
Monk, 79, 130
moral behaviour, 185
Murray and Bevan, 82
Myers, 65, 68

natural dialogue, 82, 86
natural language, 20
  processing (NLP), 69, 86
navigation, 94, 114, 116
  navigational browsing, 118
  navigational querying, 118
neighbourhood, 87
NeXT, 22
Nielsen, 47, 48
Nielsen and Lyngbaek, 74
Nordhausen, 160
Norman and Draper, 42
Norman and Rumelhart, 129
NoteCards, 94
  NoteCards browser, 102

observation, 50
Ochsman and Chapanis, 81
Olsen and Dempsey, 63
organized tours of famous
  landmarks, 179

papyrus, 187
paradigmatic examples of
  information exploration, 118
Parsaye, 73, 97, 128
partnership, 81
pattern of usage, 86
Patterson, 161
Payne, 24, 70, 90
Peckham, 21, 41
pedagogic knowledge, 112
Peridot, 65
personal affect, 149

Pew and Rollins, 59
physical space as a metaphor for
   information space, 185
planning, 153
playgrounds of the mind, 177
Popper, 43
predicted relevance, 160, 163
presentation of information, 154
Press, 81
pressure groups, 186
printing press, 187
programming by example, 65
programming by rehearsal, 65
project management, 101
prototyping, 61

quality of design, 145
   quality of instruction methods
         and guidance, 145
   quality of program, 145
   quality of training content, 145
query-encouraging questions, 125
questioning, 99
   question-and-answer, 181
   questionnaire, 143

randomly linked, 161
rapid prototyping, 61
   tools, 62
rated goodness, 48
realistic mayhem, 185
recency of use, 86
reception area, 179
reference link, 130
Reisner, 63
relevance
   relevance feedback, 135
   relevance in context, 85
religious fervour, 186
Renaissance painting, 119
rented videos, 183
Rich, 69
Ronnquist, 63
Rooms, 24, 89
Rosch, 111
Rosch and Mervis, 111

Rumelhart and Norman, 90

sadism, 185
Salomon, 85, 99
Salton, 132
Salton and McGill, 85, 113
Scapin, 81
scenario questions, 148
Schegloff and Sacks, 82
Schulert, 63
Sci-fi Village, 182
scientific explanations, 43
screen layout rules, 59
Searle, 101
selective views, 86
self generating menu system, 78
SemNet, 83
sensorium, 177
serendipity, 75
Shneiderman, 21, 41, 47, 59, 72,
   78, 123, 130
short-term store (STS), 34
Shotton, 176
Shute, 119
Simon, 39
Simpson and McKnight, 74
simulation, 153
   simulated sex, 185
Singh, 66
Singh and Green, 65
Sistine Chapel, 120
size of a building, 180
Smith, 25, 93
snapshots, 186
social conditioning, 185
sound effects, 154
space
   space warp, 95
   spatial and non-spatial
            visualizations, 84
   spatial metaphors, 80
spaghetti-like structure, 46
speech, 20
   Speech Acts, 101
Sperber and Wilson, 85
Sperling, 34
spreadsheet model, 73

starting, 134
Steve Jobs, 22
Streitz, 101
structure
    structural responsibility, 115
    structured design, 101
    structuredness, 110
students
    student attitude questionnaire,
        147, 149, 166
    students' performance, 143
    subjective opinions of students,
        143
subjects in experiments, 44
suitability, 149
summarization, 85
summative evaluation, 143
Superbook, 75, 101
surgically implanted, 175
surveys, 50
swimming through a sea of
    multimedia objects, 184
systematic arrangement, 149

target
    target orientation, 115
    target specificity, 136
task
    task analysis, 31, 49
    task relevance, 149
    task-oriented goals, 98
Taylor, 81, 82, 86
Technostress, 175
television, 183
test group, 143
Thimbleby, 59
thinking aloud, 42
Thompson and Croft, 132
three-dimensional model of
    information exploration, 115
time cars, 95
Tombaugh and McEwen, 72
transition networks, 64
transparency, 81
Trigg and Irish, 73
Turoff et al, 59
tutoring

tutor components, 153
tutorial module, 152
tutorial strategies, 112

understandability, 149
usability, 37
user interface management
    system (UIMS), 62
users in evaluations, 44

Valdez, 85
variables and control, 44
Vertelney, 61
video
    Video Night in Kathmandu, 174
    video prototypes, 61
    video recording, 50
views of the hyperbase, 96
violent combat, 185
virtual worlds, 175
visualization of structure, 83
von Kempelen, 62

Wang and Chua, 131
Wasserman, 59
Wasserman and Shewmake, 63
Waterworth, 19, 36, 82
Waterworth and Chignell, 77, 86,
    95, 113
Waterworth and Talbot, 19 82
Webs, 98
welcome screen, 129
Weyer, 74
Weyer and Borning, 92
Whalen and Patrick, 83
Whiteside, 48
WIMP interface, 69, 184
Winograd, 67
Winograd and Flores, 22, 82, 101
within-subject designs, 45
Wizard of Oz, 62
working memory, 34
workload, 149
world knowledge, 89
Wright and Lickorish, 74
writing/research, 54

Yankelovich, 119
Yoder, 77, 94

Zimmerman, 59
Zubir Said, 106